Linux for Beginners
Basic Linux Commands and Shell Scripting

Travis Booth

Books by Travis Booth

Scan the Code to Learn More

Machine Learning Series

Machine Learning With Python: Hands-On Learning for Beginners

Machine Learning With Python: An In Depth Guide Beyond the Basics

Python Data Analytics Series

Python Data Analytics: The Beginner's Real World Crash Course

Python Data Analytics: A Hands-On Guide Beyond the Basics

Python Data Science Series

Python Data Science: Hands-On Learning for Beginners

Python Data Science: A Hands-On Guide Beyond the Basics

Deep Learning Series

Deep Learning With Python: A Hands-On Guide for Beginners

Deep Learning With Python: A Comprehensive Guide Beyond the Basics

Bonus Offer: Get the Ebook absolutely free when you purchase the paperback via Kindle Matchbook!

Table of Contents

Introduction

This book contains proven steps and strategies on how to use or migrate to Linux for fun and profit. This is the first in a series of books on Linux. You can learn the basic concepts and applications of Linux from this book: from installation to basic shell scripting. The upcoming books in the series will provide you in depth knowledge of Linux concepts, philosophy and applied knowledge. The book series is well organized to provide you with sufficient knowledge as a beginner to become an advanced Linux user.

Who Should Read this Book?

This book is written in simple technical terms and uses simple examples and explanations so that a user who has zero or minimal experience with Linux can learn what Linux is and how to get started with Linux. The structure of the book is focused on providing step by step instructions and examples with screenshots and clarifications to avoid confusion and ambiguity. The content is targeting not only just for a beginner, but for general computer users, junior administrators and executives who wish to learn or sharpen what they know about Linux and how it is practically used.

How this Books is Organized and be Used

This book guides you through the initial setup of your own Linux system and moves forward with the most needed Linux system administration basics for starters. In the later chapters, it covers more advanced topics including certain system administration principles, theories and practical applications, basic and advanced scripting, and programs such as GAWK. The book is organized in the following way.

- You will learn more about Linux, history, flavors and much more (chapter 1).
- Installing and using your first Linux box and some basic administration (chapter 2).
- Linux user management principles, practical approaches, editors, terminal and console (chapter 3).
- Introduction to Linux commands, file system, and basic administration (chapter 4).
- Linux partition styles, data files, and manipulation with sorting, searching with grep, compressing/de-compressing and archiving (chapter 5).
- Shell scripting prerequisites, such as understanding processes, environment variables, and arrays (chapter 6).
- Command aliases, file descriptors, piles, mathematical operations, advanced structured commands, and examples (chapter 7).
- Introduction to functions, parameters, options, getopt and getopts, reading user input and interactive scripting, advanced functions, libraries, and a complete lesson on GAWK (chapter 8).

Tips, Notes, Caution and Scenarios

The book is designed to have many typographical features to help you get the most information from this book.

Tips: Tips are useful information and tips/tricks or tweaks on certain commands and features to make things easier.

Notes: Notes will provide you additional information about certain commands, decisions and outputs so that

Caution: Provides you warnings about commands and bugs.

Scenario: This will indicate a scenario in an explanation or an example

Why Linux?

Linux is an open-source operating system or a kernel. It is not only the most popular server operating system, but also the widely used open-source operating system. It was founded by Linus Torvalds in 1991 with the collaboration of GNU. Linux is used to power a multitude of systems. For instance, laptops, computers, smartphones, smart refrigerators and many more. Even though in the beginning, it was only famous in computer programmers, now it is used almost everywhere. Today Linux servers run Google, Facebook and many other well-known services.

Linux is different when compared to other popular clients operating systems such as Windows and Mac OS. Linux is an open-source system while other systems are not. That means users cannot make changes in those operating systems since the user cannot access their source code. But anyone can modify the Linux operating system. This does not mean Linux does not have commercial editions.

Some refer to Linux as a clone of UNIX. UNIX was the foundation of Linux, or technically speaking an inspiration in terms of technology. When considering the core both are similar. Even though Linux is like UNIX it has its unique features. Some of the differences between UNIX and Linux are:

- Linux is very flexible, but UNIX is rigid, hence it cannot be used in any computer.
- Linux offers extensive portability in contrast to Unix.
- Source code of Linux is readily available, but for UNIX is it is not actually the case.

These are the reasons for the foundation of Linux.

A complete Linux system package can be called distribution. This includes the Linux kernel, GNU applications, a desktop environment and applications. There are so many available distributions addressing a plethora of needs. Some of the noteworthy distributions are:

- Linux Mint.
- Ubuntu.
- Debian.
- Red Hat/Cent OS.
- Fedora.
- SUSE.
- Kali.

These distributions are customized for users' needs. One can choose the most suitable distribution according to their needs. For instance, Ubuntu can be installed easily, and anyone can use it, while OpenSUSE requires advanced knowledge. Some distributions, such as Linux Mint, can use who has low computer expertise.

Recently there is a surge of Linux users due to many benefits. When considering the benefits of Linux, the most popular one is that it is free. Since operating systems, such as Windows and Mac are quite expensive, Linux has become predominant among users. Although in the history Linux was not a user-friendly operating system, now it has sufficient facilities and users can choose from millions of applications. It is flexible and highly customizable. One can install what he/she wants without downloading a full set of features.

One of the major benefits of Linux is its security. Since there many severe problems have arisen due to security issues with many operating systems, the increased use of Linux is inevitable, given its strong security architecture. When using Linux, it is not necessary to use anti-virus programs in most cases (this does not mean it is entirely free of bugs or vulnerabilities, but these are rare). It is also beneficial when considering user privacy because the Linux system does not collect details of the user.

Since Linux is an open-source operating system, any enthusiast has the opportunity modify a distribution. It gives the opportunity to make one's own Linux distribution. Even with all these facilities, it is highly stable and reliable.

Installation of Linux is extremely simplified now with modern GUI capabilities, and it works on almost every hardware. Software updates and patches also are faster when compared to other operating systems. The support teams available for general Linux users, as well as the enterprise users, is becoming ever popular.

Linux also had a few disadvantages. The main reason for this was Linux was not a dominant operating system in the market. Therefore, users had to face some difficulties, such as:

- Most of the drivers are written for Windows or Mac OS X. Therefore, some hardware cannot be used with Linux for advanced operations. This is especially true when it comes to gaming.

- Finding support services is difficult when compared to other operating systems
- It is quite difficult to find popular applications.
- Certain major vendors have not developed priority software for Linux because Linux was not a popular client operating system, such as Windows or Mac.

In addition to the afore-mentioned disadvantages there are few other issues. One is the number of flavors of Linux. It is extensive. This may confuse beginners. Since Linux offers more control to the user, newbies may experience a difficult time. When considering users whose main focus is gaming, they might not be satisfied with Linux due to it is the limitation with popular gaming applications and certain driver support issues.

Even though Windows operating system is dominant for the past few decades, Linux has gained popularity at present. There are several advantages to Linux when compared to the operating systems such as Windows. A few of those are:

- Linux offers more secure and an error free environment, given the security architecture and nature of the applications.
- Linux still runs on decades old computers.
- With Linux, advanced user can make operating system level changes while the others do not allow such modifications.
- A person who works on a Mac can easily adapt Linux when compared to Windows because the Mac operating system also uses a UNIX like operating system.

Since Linux offers more versatility to the users, most of the famous platforms, such as android phones, use Linux. The following is a list of industry and tech giants relying on Linux based devices for their mission critical applications.

- Google
- Facebook
- Twitter
- Amazon
- NASA
- McDonald's

CERN, World's largest Physics laboratory uses Linux to power its **hardon collider** (particle accelerator). More than 90% of world supercomputers run on Linux. There are countless other instances. The internet is dominated by Linux flavors.

Even proprietary platforms release their editions for Linux, drivers and other developments focused on Linux. This helps to provide reliability, flexibility and scalability. For instance, companies like Steam release operating systems based on Linux to offer console-like experience in living rooms.

There are many job prospects when considering the Linux platform. The cloud uses Linux extensively. DevOps and SysOps areas are gaining speed with Linux. Many industry applications use Linux for mega projects. Many sectors, such as education, healthcare, IT and military, adapt and enhance it in multiple ways. It is time to move on with Linux!

At the end of this book you will gain a comprehensive knowledge to operate your own Linux machine with confident. Ready to step in and get your hands dirty?

CHAPTER 1: Introduction to Linux Kernel and Operating System

In this chapter you will learn:

> What Linux Is
>
> Linux Kernel
>
> Distributions of Linux
>
> Linux Desktop System
>
> GNU
>
> Shell

Everything starts with a proper introduction. In this chapter, we will look into Linux from an operating system perspective.

What is Linux?

Without going into assumptions that you know everything about an operating system, let's briefly look into the terms and definitions a bit. Then we will try to understand what Linux is and its architecture.

An operating system is a software program that has the purpose of proving a better way to interact with a bundle of hardware, or what we call a computer. It provides many ways to utilize a set of integrated and interoperable hardware by communicating, managing, and maintaining itself, including hardware, as a set of application programs. Without an operating system, the computer mindless (not a brain, but a mind, since the process can be thought of as the brain). If we take a more traditional definition, the operating system is an interface between the user and the hardware or the combination of electronic devices that we call peripherals. The operating system usually gets loaded into the memory during the boot (startup) process of a computer and it basically diagnoses the health of the entire system, then loads the interactivity feature so that a user can interact. It is responsible for memory management and process management, loading, unloading things from a hard disk to memory and other complex things. It is also responsible for recovery processes.

Now you know what an operating system is and how important its role. There are many operating systems in use nowadays and the major operating systems are Unix, Linux, Windows, and Mac OS. Now when it comes to one of the popular operating systems, such as Windows, it is clear what an operating system is. It is propriety and clearly distinguishable. However, when it comes to Unix and Linux, there is more to learn about the origin and how the differences came into reality.

If you are an enthusiastic about the history of the operating systems, Unix is one of the oldest operating systems, especially for server systems. It was a derivative of an even older system called "Multics". In 1970, Ken Thompson rewrote this small system in C with Dennis Ritchie, who developed the C programming language. Unix grew quickly in academia and Berkeley was the center of it. They introduced the Berkeley Software Distribution or BSD. During the 70s and 80s, Unix evolved as an operating system outside the academy and was adopted by other organizations. There were flavors, like IBM-AIX, HP-UX, Sun Solaris, etc. An important thing to remember is that Unix wasn't an open source software. Eventually, under the BSD family, some open source variants emerged, such as FreeBSD. This licensing is now known as BSD License.

Linux came into the existence thanks to the effort of two important names. Richard Stallman and Linus Torvalds. During 90s, Richard was willing to create a truly open source and free alternative to proprietary Unix systems. He was creating a collection of utilities and programs under the name GNU. GNU is a recursive acronym and it stands for "GNU's is Not Unix!". However, a set of programs and utilities won't work with a kernel!

What is a Kernel? Kernel is the core of an operating system. It has the complete control over the entire computer once booted into. It may be loaded by a small loading program and then it is the alpha and omega. It is loaded into the same or separate memory space, and then controls and assigns the hardware, controls input/output operations, software requests and processing. During the time at the University of Helsinki, Linus was creating a non-operating system specific program so that he can use his new PC with the specific processor that existed during those days. He was using GNU C compiler and some other tools, and the development carried on MINIX (although the architecture changed from microkernel to a monolithic kernel). Thanks to Linus and his relationship with GNU, Linux was born as a usable operating system and Richard's free and opensource dream became a reality.

Linux is a Unix-like operating system. We could also say it is a clone of Unix in some way. Linux basically is comprised of the Kernel, GNU, X-Windows GUI, and a Graphical Desktop system. It includes other applications and utilities as well.

The Role of the Kernel

Since we started with an introduction into the kernel, let's look at some more technical details. This will help you to understand some important aspects of Linux, as well as other operating systems.

Linux occupies a monolithic kernel. In other words, it uses the same address space to manage memory, files, processes, etc. This makes the kernel faster than the microkernel. It is also easier to manage. The only drawback is the bottleneck it creates as a single space of failure. However, the modern operating systems have overcome such issues and Linux distributions are highly robust, reliable, stable and secure operating systems.

Linux kernel is responsible for the following tasks.

- Process management.

- Scheduling.

- Inter-process communication.

- Memory management.

- File System management.

- Device and driver management (hardware).

- Network management.

- Security.

We will be looking into this deeper when we discuss the related topics during this series. For now, let's look at how these things are arranged.

Since we are looking into Linux, let's get an idea of versioning. Versioning is a critical part of any software development. Linux kernel, as well as any distribution, has a version number. It has the following format.

<Major Number><Minor Number><Micro Number>-<Patch Level>

The version represents the version number. The release can be an even or an odd number. The even number represents a stable release, while the odd number indicates a version in development. The patch level is also important here. It indicates the bugfixes.

Any Linux distribution has its own versioning. If we take few examples:

- The latest Ubuntu version is 18.04. The upcoming version is 19.04.

- Latest Red Hat release is 8.0 and the kernel version is 4.18.0-80.

This formatting is subject to change at any time.

Linux Kernel Releases and Support
There are 4 release types.

- Pre-patch: These are RC (release candidate) versions targeting developers and enthusiasts.

- Mainline: This is managed by Linus and the developers and is the root of development. Major releases occur per 2 – 3 months.

- Stable: Once the mainline release is out and bugs are fixed, it is considered stable. It is maintained by a designated custodian. There may be a few bug releases until the next release. These updates often occur on a weekly basis.

- Long-term: Some flavors arrive with long term support. For instance, the distribution is maintained and patched at least for a couple of years. This line of distribution is known as Long-Term Support or LTS. However, older trees are not patched very often.

It is worth mentioning the release of other kernels by Linux distributors. Major Linux flavor developers release their own long-term support distributions. These are not maintained by the main line, but rather by the distributor individually through their own support channel.

To find more about kernels, visit https://www.kernel.org/

Linux LBS

Standardization is vital for any operating system or a software platform to maintain interoperability and compatibility. For instance, compiled software should be capable of (compatible) running on any Linux platform. Like POSIX, LBS is a specification that appears to define services and Application Binary Interfaces (ABIs). However, some distributors may not align themselves with this standard.

Linux Distributions

A Linux distribution or a "distro" is a complete Linux package consisting of the kernel and other components we discussed. There are many distributors who integrate and distribute these so that end-users do not have to do anything complex.

According to https://distrowatch.com/ currently there are 288 Linux distributions and it is gradually declining. peaked at 323 and now it is 288.

These distributions are specific, or targeting a specific user group, or a functional group, such as developers, infrastructure, multimedia, or even general users. Let's look at 3 major types of distributions.

- Core distributions.

- Special distributions.

- Live CDs.

Most applications are customized for desktop users and business users. It includes facilities to install and use Linux easier, popular operating system-like desktop distributions, (e.g., similar to Windows or Mac) and autodetection/configuration of hardware. These distributions made Linux revolutionary popular among desktop users.

Major Linux Distributions

Slackware	Patrick Volkerding created Slackware during 1992 and is the oldest surviving Linux distro. It is famous for the bug-free and clean distributions. It runs on both 32-bit (i486) and 64-bit (x86_64) architectures. The philosophy is similar to Arch Linux. There are few drawbacks, such as a limited number of application support and upgrade complexities.
Debian	GNU/Linux came to existence on 1993. Today Debian can be thought of as the largest Linux distro and largest possible collaborative software project. According to Distrowatch, Debian is developed by more than 1000 volunteers, 50000+ binary packages, and inspiring over 120 distros. Debian is highly stable, has an outstanding quality assurance and supports the most processor architectures in contrast to others. One of the main drawbacks is the release of stable updates (2-3 years).
Fedora	Fedora is one of the most innovative Linux distros at present. It is linked to the famous Red Hat Linux. On 2003, Red Hat introduced a revolutionary change: the Fedora Core. It is introduced as a community edition designed for Linux hobbyists. Right now, Red Hat is the most profitable enterprise. Fedora presents outstanding security, supports multiple desktop environments, contributed to the kernel advancements, glibc and GCC, SELinux integration, journaled file system, system and other enterprise features. It also supports both 32-bit and 64-bit environments. It is geared toward more enterprise features and users.
Red Hat and Cent OS	Red Hat holds the flagship in the enterprise. It started in 1995. It had many innovative components, such as Anaconda GIU-based installer, RPM package manager, and more. Regrettably, it failed to maintain its phase with rising patent issues and similar. It ended its life on 2003 and gave birth to RHEL (Red Hat Enterprise Linux) and Fedora core. RHEL is undoubtedly the industry de-facto. It is able to operate on platforms like x86_64, Arm64, Power ISA, IBM Z and desktop platforms. It has huge variations targeting different enterprise-class applications such as servers and workstations. In the meantime, Fedora works as the upstream for future RHEL versions. Given the leadership and influence, exceptional support, cutting edge technology, RHEL is a superb for the enterprise use. It is used by tech giants.

Gentoo	Gentoo is a highly flexible meta distribution which allows users to run a verity of kernels and software configurations. Gentoo can be customized. This project introduced by Daniel Robbins in 2000. Even though it offers flexibility, it requires expertise to use. In other words, this is not suitable for inexperienced users, as it may take more time to get used to it. The upgrades can be time-consuming.
Arch Linux	Arch Linux was launched by Judd Vinet in 2002. In the beginning, it was considered as a marginal project that existed between intermediate and advanced users. Later on, it was promoted using a feature called "rolling- release". Rolling-release means the operation system has the ability to keeps itself up to date. Arch Linux has an excellent software management infrastructure. It is included the ability to install software from the source code. One of the disadvantages is the risk of breakdown due to occasional instabilities.
Ubuntu	Ubuntu revolutionizes Linux for desktop users. It has been popular for a long time. It was launched in 2004 and is still popular among Linux Users. Ubuntu is based on DEB packages. It has a long-term support via Canonical and it even supports the enterprise now with its server edition. Some special features of Ubuntu are that it includes an installable live DVD, it supports for new technologies where a novice can easily get used to Ubuntu and the different desktop environments. One of the Significant disadvantages of Ubuntu is its lack of compatibility.

MX Linux	MX Linux was introduced as a replacement for MEPIS Linux. This has designed for personal purposes as well as business. The most popular feature of MX Linux is its graphical administrative tools, known as MX-Tools. It also has exceptional support for the platform, exceptional compatibility with graphics drivers and the ease of administration. MX Linux may not be friendly for novices when compared Mint and Ubuntu. It takes time to get used to it and its installer and some tools may appear different.
Mint	Linux Mint was launched in 2006. It was designed based on Ubuntu. This distribution is the best for the beginners. Mint has a wide range of enhancements that make it user friendly. It provides interoperability with other operating systems. Therefore, it is suitable not only for personal use, but also for the enterprise. The developers offer 3 types of releases namely official (on December), point releases (as needed, e.g., bug fixes) and a monthly snapshot release. This makes Mint highly stable.
Backtrack and Kali	There are other special Linux editions geared toward system security and penetration. Kali Linux is the most popular penetration testing platform at present. It all started with the creation of BackTrack from the merger of WHAX (WHAX was a Slax based Linux distribution. The company that was behind this was **Offensive Security**. Earlier versions of WHAX was based on Knoppix and named Whoppix). BackTrack 5 was based on Ubuntu Lucid LTS. It supported both 32-bit and 64-bit architectures and ARM. In 2013, the company rebuilt the platform based on Debian and released in under the name Kali. Kali Linux is highly stable and advanced with its capabilities and the set of top-level penetration testing tools.

What about Android? Android is the largest distribution based on a modified version of the Linux kernel, and Google's own libraries. Android also runs a virtual platform called Dalvin to run the applications written in Java. Such applications target different hardware platform and it depends on the Google APIs. You cannot run a desktop version of Linux in an Android device. You cannot run a mobile Android version in a PC (without emulation and virtualization).

Linux Live CDs

Linux Live CDs and USBs are quite popular among a variety of users. It goes beyond simply learning what Linux is before the installation. Many Linux live distributions support running an operating system from a CD ROM. It is great for demonstration purposes and to test out things. The customized distributions include packages to carry out various simple and complex system tasks, such as changing hard disk layouts, security and recovery procedures and many more. These versions are now appearing as Linux Live USB distributions. The site https://livecdlist.com/ lists a huge collection of live CDs. All the major distributions support the live CD functionality.

Linux Live CD Distributions

Puppy Linux Puppy Linux is a small system that is less than 200MB. This Linux distribution is best for basic computer functions and web browsing. Even though it is ultra-small, file recovery tools and partitioning are still available. This distribution makes it easy to install other popular applications because it has its own package manager. Puppy Linux has various customized versions known as "puplets". One of the advantages of the Puppy Linux is it can be used in older hardware.

Slax Slax is a small and fast Linux distribution. It was based on Slackware. But now it's based on Debian stable. It is one of the user-friendly Linux distribution. Users can delete or add modules when downloading. Slax is quite convenient. This distribution can be booted by different media such as USB flash or DVD ROM. Slax have a boot menu which includes many options.

Knoppix Knoppix Is a stable Linux distribution. It is one of the very first Linux CDs. This is well established and has over 1000 software packages. One of the advantages of Knoppix is, it supports distinctive hardware. Even though Knoppix is aimed to run from live media it can also be installed into a hard drive. There are many derivatives of Knoppix.

Tiny Core Linux	Tiny Core Linux distribution is a very small portable operating system. It is only 10MB. Since this operation system is very small, it does not include applications or a file manager. However, users can install them later. This is one of the recommended options for beginners.
Ubuntu	Ubuntu does not have a specific LiveCD. However, its ISO image can be burned onto a DVD or set up into a USB as bootable. It has an option to try upon booting from it.
MX Linux	MX Linux is suitable for both older and modern computers. This is a user-friendly distribution and novice can use this.

The Linux Desktop System

Linux desktop was a basic command line or text interface in the beginning. With the evolution of client operating systems such as Windows, there was more demand for a well-organized GUI. Now there are multiple graphical desktops to select from. The Linux graphical environment consists of a system software, such as the X-Windows system, and on top of it there is a desktop environment. Let's first look at the X-Windows.

The X-Windows System

The main hardware responsible for graphical environment in your PC is the monitor and the graphics card/driver. Any operating system if supports graphical environment, must communicate with both first. In Linux it is the responsibility of the X-Windows system. This is a low-level system program communicating and managing the processes to create an environment where graphical environment can be created. This is what the X-Windows system does in a Linux operating system and is based on a client/server architecture – X server is responsible for handling the graphics request from any clients (e.g., applications). Therefore, it supported network protocols (initially, the communication was insecure, however). This system was developed at MIT.

During the installation of Linux, it will detect the monitor and the graphics card and then an X-Windows configuration file will be created. This is easier to spot during an installation, as the screen may turn Black and may blink a few times.

With the development, this older system evolved into more modern editions. The XFree86 and X.org editions.

The XFRee86 is one of the volunteer organization expanding the free and opensource X-Windows system. Unix, Linux systems, BSD variants, Sun Solaris, and some Mac OS systems run this distribution.

The other player is X.org (part of the Open Group). It took the old X-Windows system to new heights and is now popular among the two. You can find out more at https://www.x.org/wiki/

Types of Desktop Environments

The X-Windows system can construct the base, but to run a complete desktop environment another program must run it because X-Windows system is not useful when it comes to regular users who depend on a GUI all the time.

In order to enable the full featured desktop environment, another set of programs exist. These are known as the **Desktop Environments**. Let's have a look at some of the popular environments.

KDE Desktop

KDE or the K Desktop Environment is one of the older and popular systems, even now. It gained the popularity because it was similar to the Microsoft Windows desktop environment. KDE is not just an environment. It is also a collection of applications. It is also highly customizable.

The latest versions have two variations called Plasma Desktop and Plasma Notebook. Unlike other desktops KDE offer a full set of applications and experience (you can get a full list here: https://kde.org/applications/). Major Linux platforms, such as OpenSUSE and Kubuntu use this as the default. Here is a list of KDE applications (version 19.04).

- **Amarok**: Music Player
- **Dolphin**: File manager.
- **Dragon Player**: Video player.
- **Kate**: Development environment.
- **Kmail**: Email with privacy protection.
- **Konsole**: KDE terminal emulator.
- **KOrganizer**: Contact manager.
- **KWrite**: Text editor.
- **Okular**: Universal document viewer.
- **Spectacle**: Screenshot application.

GNOME

GNOME was first released in 1999. GNOME stands for GNU Network Object Model Environment. It is another extremely popular desktop environment. However, for the user who depends on Windows-like desktop, GNOME has a different taste. It moved away from the

Windows look and yet incorporates many similar features. If you are familiar with Ubuntu, this is the desktop you have to deal with most of the time.

Among the similarities, the desktop icons, Windows-like panels (at the top and bottom), menus and drag-drop capabilities are available. However, there is a lack of application for GNOME desktop. To handle this obstacle, the Linux distributions that use GNOME, incorporates KDE libraries. The latest GNOME interface has some similarities to Mac OS if you are familiar with Mac systems.

GNOME offers the following applications. You can get a full list of applications from here: https://wiki.gnome.org/Apps/

- **Empathy**: A universal messenger app.
- **Evince**: Document viewer.
- **Geary**: GNOME mail client. Evolution is a similar application with calendar and an address-book.
- **Gedit**: Text editor.
- **Gnome-terminal**: Terminal emulator.

Other popular desktop environments are in the list below.

- **MATE**: MATE is somewhat traditional in its look and feel with a hint of modernism. It was developed based on GNOME 2. Ubuntu MATE is an operating system that uses MATE. More information is available at https://mate-desktop.org/
- **XFCE**: Xfce stands for **XFOrms Common Environment**. This is a light-weight desktop environment which consumes low resources, user-friendly and visual appealing. It is somewhat similar to the GNOME desktop because it is based on the GTK toolkit. However, it is not a GNOME fork. It is available for both Unix and Linux distributions. MX Linux, Manjaro and Xubuntu use this desktop environment. More information is available at https://www.xfce.org/
- **LXDE**: This stands for Lightweight X11 Desktop Environment. As the name implies, it is faster and lighter, yet has a feature rich environment. It has a good set of applications and an active community. LXDE is a great desktop environment for older computers. This had a similar look to GNOME, but it is transforming. The reason behind its GNOME look and feel is the use of GTK +2 toolkit. This also runs on Unix and Linux platforms. Lubuntu, Knoppix, Peppermint operating systems use LXDE as their desktop environment. More information is available at https://lxde.org/

GNU Utilities

I introduced GNU and the relationship it had with Linux kernel. You may have seen the use of GNU/Linux term. Now you know the reason behind it. GNU was designed for Unix people to experience a Unix-like environment. This is why the set of utilities include many Unix-like command line utilities.

Linux system uses a set of core utilities and is known as **coreutils**. It includes the utilities to manage file, shell and text manipulation. Every GNU/Linux distribution should include these core utilities. The most important one among these is the **Shell**. In the next chapter we will look into the shell in more detail. The following is an introduction to the shell.

The Shell

Shell is basically a program that takes keyboard input to the operating system to process. It is an interactive utility. Shell supports functions such as file management, execute/manage programs, and processes. The core component of the shell is the command prompt.

The shell provides the access to its internal commands so that a user can perform actions on files, such as creating and deleting. Furthermore, it provides the ability to execute and end programs.

You can create a program using a set of shell commands. We call this **"shell scripting"**. We will be looking at this in detail in the next chapters.

CHAPTER 2: Installing Linux

In this chapter you will learn:

Installing Linux

UEFI vs Legacy BIOS

System Requirements

Post-installation Tasks

Troubleshooting

Installing Linux

With the evolution of Linux distributions, there have been radical changes to the graphical interfaces and utilities. Installing Linux is much easier than in 90s. This does not mean it cannot be installed via command line. It can be a personal preference or probably an industry requirement. For an example, both the setting up a server and reduce the attack surface can be achieved through command line installation. We will look into both the methods in this chapter. Let's start with the system requirements.

There are 288 Linux distributions and the installation methods can be different. I am not expecting to cover all the installation methods, as it is not the intention of the book. We will look into the installation of Ubuntu as it is quite popular and useful.

Trying a Live CD first

If you are expecting to install a Linux operating system as a bear metal installation you can install it straightaway. However, if you want to try it out first or do a demonstration of its use, you can first run it as a Live CD. This mode is supported by most Linux distributions.

In this series, we will be using both Ubuntu and Red Hat or Cento OS to provide examples.

Let's learn how to prepare Ubuntu Live CD first.

1. Download Ubuntu from http://www.ubuntu.com/getubuntu/download
2. In a Windows or a Linux platform, burn the ISO image to a DVD.
3. Boot from the DVD and select "Try Ubuntu".

If you want to create a USB there are instructions. The steps also provide the guide to set up a DVD in step 13). If you do not have an operating system installed, you have to boot into "Try without installing". Then you can use the Gparted partition tool, for instance, if you want to create a USB stick to boot a computer.

1. You need to use a USB with 4 GB capacity. Remember that your USB will be erased during the set up. If the USB stick is a USB 3.0 it will be faster.
2. The USB stick must support booting. There may be some sticks with problems. This must be verified before selecting a USB.
3. If you are on Windows, you can use a software, such as Rufus, to prepare the USB and complete the installation. Since we are learning Linux, why don't we do it on Linux?
4. On a Linux system, let's use Gparted to create the USB stick. I am using Ubuntu to create the USB. If you are using a Live CD, it is already there.
5. Let's install gparted with the following command:
   sudo apt-get install gparted
6. Format the USB once.
7. Press Ctrl+H to show hidden files. Load the image file (mount) to USB (copy).
8. Right click on the partition, select Manage Flags and enable *boot* and *lba* flags.

If you want to use something else, like mkusb:

1. To structure and format let's use a utility called *mkusb*. First let's obtain it on Ubuntu (standard edition). Press enter at each line.
   sudo add-apt-repository universe
   sudo add-apt-repository ppa:mkusb/ppa
   sudo apt-get update
   sudo apt-get install mkusb
2. For ease let's use the GUI version of mkusb.
3. Run the tool and examine the options. You can restore the USB to a standard storage device after the process.

Image: mkusb utility

4. From the first option you can create a bootable device. It will wipe the first megabyte and create the require layout.

If you would like to use usb-creator on Ubuntu

1. To create the portable USB from the ISO you obtained, let's use usb-creator utility in Ubuntu. Simply mount the USB and start this program.

2. For the source image, provide the image by browsing to the path. This is if the image is not listed – if it is not, use the *Other...* button to find it.
3. Disk to use: Select the USB stick from the list. You can insert a DVD if you want to use a DVD instead.
4. If you use USB, select the first bootable partition from the list. The partition should be in Fat16 or FAT32 format.
5. If you get a Dbus error, please refer https://bugs.launchpad.net/usb-creator/+bug/458334

What if your computer is utilizing UEFI?

It is easier to install Ubuntu if the BIOS mode is set to legacy. If it is a UEFI (Unified Extensible Firmware Install), you need to setup a UEFI mode boot device. USB is the best option here.

You do not have to install Linux in UEFI mode unless there is another system installed and you want to install in a dual-boot configuration.

1. Obtain Ubuntu 64bit ISO. It is better to obtain version 12.10 or higher, as these versions support secure boot technology.
2. When you create your USB stick, use Gparted, as instructed above.
3. Access your computer's firmware menu and disable Quickboot/Fastboot and Intel Smart Response Technology (SRT). If you are using a Windows 8 or higher, disable Fast Startup.
4. Set up your firmware to boot from UEFI mode. That is all!

Booting from your Live CD

1. Insert the DVD or the USB stick and turn on the computer.
2. Select the language.
3. When you are prompted with options, select "Try Ubuntu without any change to your computer".

Linux System Requirements for Major Distributions

The following table lists the recommended requirements for the following Linux distributions. There are not the minimum requirements! These are the recommended requirements. Why are minimum requirements removed from this table? Because at present, people use generally powerful computers with newer hardware. Having a computer with at least 1 GB memory and at least 40-80 GB hard disk is extremely likely. Therefore, the minimum and somewhat unrealistic requirements are not deliberately included. If you wish to find out what those are, please refer the manufacturer's website or the knowledge-base.

Table: Linux System Requirements for Major Distributions

Linux Distribution	CPU	Memory	Hard Disk
Red Hat Linux 7	Intel/AMD 64, ARM and more	768MiB – 1.5 GiB	10 GiB
Cent OS 7	I386, x86_64, PowerPC8le, IA-32, ARMv7hl, AARch64 (arm64) 1 GB logical CPU for 64bit	1 GB	10-20 GB
Mint 19.1	64bit recommended	2 GB	20 GB
Ubuntu 18.04.3	2 GHz Dual-core	2 GB	25 GB
Fedora 30	2 GHz	4 GB	10-20 GB
Debian 9	2 GHz	2 GiB	25 GiB
MX Linux	i486	2 GB	5 GB
Kali Linux			

Performing a Basic GUI Installation

1. Insert the bootable media and restart the computer. If you are using a virtual machine, simply mount the ISO file into the DC/DVD ROM and start the virtual machine.
2. *You will see the boot menu first.*
3. Next, you have to decide whether you want to try or install Ubuntu. Click *Install Ubuntu*.
4. Next, select or change your keyboard layout and click continue.
5. In the next screen you will be presenter with 4 options.
    a. Normal installation (similar to a full feature installation).
    b. Minimum installation, which includes browser and a minimal set of utilities. This is good for security purposes.

c. Other options: Download updates while installing Ubuntu - This option will update your system during the installation. However, this will take more time. You can even do this once you install the system.
d. Other options: Install third-party software for graphics and Wi-Fi hardware and additional media formats – This option is important. If your computer requires additional drivers, you can install it with this option.

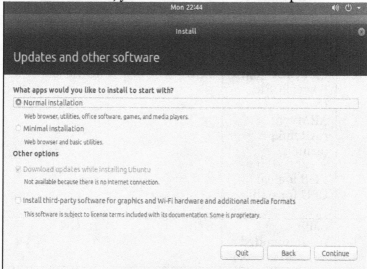

Image: Ubuntu install options

6. Next is the disk options. You will get 4 options here.
    a. Erase disk and install Ubuntu: Do not ever use this option if you are preparing for a dual-boot configuration. Otherwise, this is the best option.
    b. Encrypt: You can enable encryption during the installation.
7. Use LVM: This option enables you to utilize the Logical Volume Manager. It helps disk management tasks, such as resizing partitions and taking snapshots so that you can recover the OS later.

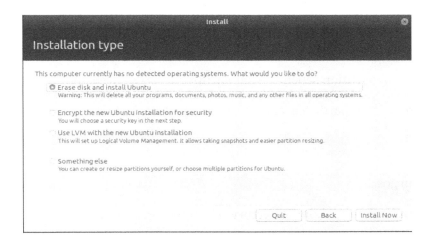

Image: Ubuntu installation type

8. If you want to keep dual-boot configuration or set up a new partition table, click *Something else*. It will take you to a new screen.

Image: Ubuntu partition options

Ubuntu and Linux systems display the hard disks as files. If the disk was an IDE, the names will be /dev/hda to /dev/hdd. For SCSi controllers, it is /dev/sda. If there were more disks, they will be named as /dev/sda, /dev/sdb etc. And the partitions will be

/dev/sda1, /dev/sda2 etc. You can use MBR or GPT as the partition style. The latter is the new scheme and it provides multiple advantages over MBR. GPT or GUID partition table sets a unique GUID for each partition, the number of partitions are virtually unlimited and it is solid against data corruption. On EFI and UEFI systems GPT is used.

9. If you are to create a custom partition scheme, what partitions are required and what are the size requirements?
    a. Linux has different set of partitions and let's have a look at the table below.

Table: Linux directories

Directory	Purpose
/	This is the root home directory. The upper-most level.
/bin	This is the binary store. GNU utilities (user-level) exist in this directory.
/boot	This is where the system stores the boot directory and files used during the boot process.
/dev	Device directory and nodes.
/etc	This is where the system stores the configuration files.
/home	Home of user directories.
/lib	System and application libraries.
/media	This is where media is mounted, media such as CDs, USB drives.
/mnt	Where the removable media is mounted to.
/opt	Optional software packages are stored here.
/proc	Process information – not open for users.
/root	Home directory of root.
/sbin	System binary store. Administrative utilities are stored here.
/tmp	This is the place for temporary files.

/usr	This is where the user-installed software are stored.
/var	Variable director where the dynamic files such as logs are stored.

When you create a specific partition scheme you need to consider the following calculations.

/boot: if the disk is more than 100 GB.	**250 – 1000 MB**
/SWAP	At least the size of the RAM
/	Minimum 8 GB to 15 GB

For GPT and EFI partitions, a BIOS boot partition (for Legacy Boot) or an EFI partition is required. If legacy, this partition is 1 MB in size. And if EFI it has to be mounted at /boot/efi and the size is 100-250 MB (fat32).

SWAP is a virtual memory reserved for memory operations. If the system requires more memory space, inactive areas or pages are dumped or swapped with disk. SWAP must not be thought of as a replacement for memory. The old rule for SWAP size is 2 x RAM. However, this is no longer true.

Table: Linux SWAP partition recommendations

Memory Size Installed	SWAP Space	SWAP with Hibernation
<=2 GB	2 x RAM	3 x RAM
2 - 8 GB	= RAM	2 x RAM
8 – 64 GB	4 GB to ½ x RAM (8 GB is sufficient)	1.5 x RAM
> 64 GB	4 GB	Hibernation should be avoided

The following is a recommended custom partition scheme found on Ubuntu documentation. Since we installed Ubuntu, you can consider the following if you plan to use it for a long time.

Table: Ubuntu partition recommendation

Partition	Recommended Size
/home	All – separate disk is also better.
/usr	10 GB
/var	2 GB
/lib	5 GB
/boot	250 MB
/opt	500 MB – 5 GB. Allocation of several GBs if you use universal repositories.
/etc	250 MB
/sbin	250 MB
/bin	250 MB
/dev	Avoid partitioning
/srv	<=100 MB. If you run a web server or similar, plan it well.
/tmp	<= SWAP
/mnt	
/media	

Source: https://help.ubuntu.com/community/DiskSpace

10. Now you know how to allocate partitions. If you did not allocate any, but use the defaults, you will get the following popup.

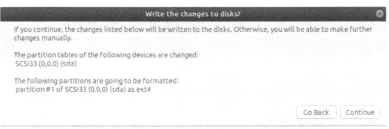

Image: Confirming the changes to the disk

11. Next, select where you are geographically located.
12. Create your user account in the next Window. An important thing to remember, especially for Windows user. Linux file system is **case-sensitive**! You must use capital and simple letters carefully. If you use a username John and john, they are not the same! This is true for files, folders and other things too.

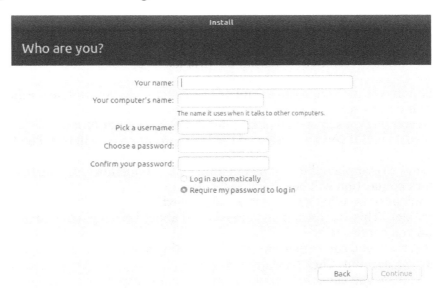

Image: Creating the first user

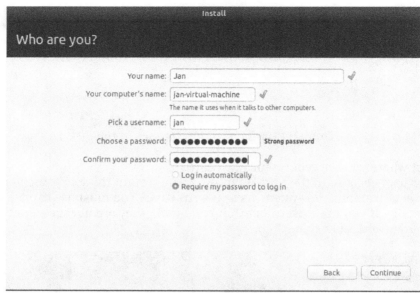

Image: Creating the first user - options

13. The installation will start once you complete these steps and you will be notified when the installation is complete.
14. Installation completion screen will be displayed. Click **Restart Now**.
15. Once you restart and if you have selected the login prompt, you will be taken to the login page.
16. Next, you have to complete the post installation tasks. Remember, during the installation, your network connection will be configured.
17. After you look into the What's new section, click Next.
18. Set up LivePatch. This is critical if you are worried about kernel patch fixing and I recommend you configure it.
19. In the next screen, you can register for this by creating a new account or sign in if you already have an account. Click Next.
20. In the next screen, you can join their anonymous quality assurance program (e.g., collecting crash data etc.,) by clicking *Help improve Ubuntu - Yes, send system info to Canonical.* If you do not want to participate, select the other option and close the window.

Welcome to your new Ubuntu workspace. This is Ubuntu 18.04.3.

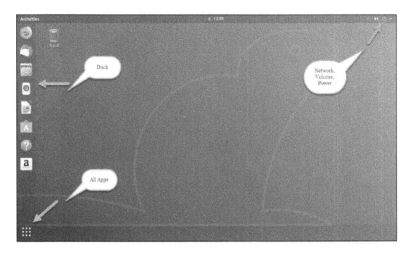

Image: Ubuntu Workspace

Post Installation Tasks

Connecting to a network

If you are unable to connect to a network, we can configure it using the GUI. To start, click the network icon at the upper-right hand corner. It will open the settings panel and then within it, the Network panel.

You simply need to go to the IPv4 section and configure it. If it is set to DHCP, in most cases you are good to go. If you are using a virtual machine, you will have to bridge the networks in the virtual machine host.

To select a manual address, do the following procedure.

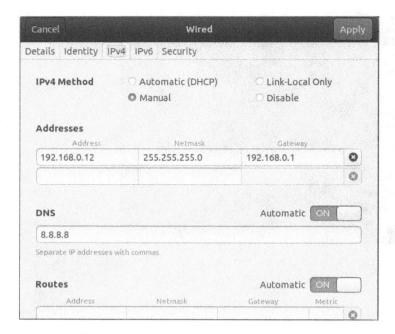

Image: Ubuntu network configuration

In addition, you can set an IPv6 address, DNS (here I use Google DNS) and other details. The wireless connection is similar to this.

How do you configure a connection using commands?

1. Right click on desktop and click *Open terminal*. The terminal helps you to execute commands and do much more. Let's learn it by getting the hands dirty.
2. You can use 2 commands to see the connection properties of the available connections.
    a. ip command –

```
jan@jan-virtual-machine: ~
File Edit View Search Terminal Help
jan@jan-virtual-machine:~$ ip a
1: lo: <LOOPBACK,UP,LOWER_UP> mtu 65536 qdisc noqueue state UNKNOWN group defaul
t qlen 1000
    link/loopback 00:00:00:00:00:00 brd 00:00:00:00:00:00
    inet 127.0.0.1/8 scope host lo
       valid_lft forever preferred_lft forever
    inet6 ::1/128 scope host
       valid_lft forever preferred_lft forever
2: ens33: <BROADCAST,MULTICAST,UP,LOWER_UP> mtu 1500 qdisc fq_codel state UP gro
up default qlen 1000
    link/ether 00:0c:29:08:60:4d brd ff:ff:ff:ff:ff:ff
    inet 192.168.0.12/24 brd 192.168.0.255 scope global noprefixroute ens33
       valid_lft forever preferred_lft forever
    inet6 fe80::b02c:2218:f6db:ab01/64 scope link noprefixroute
       valid_lft forever preferred_lft forever
jan@jan-virtual-machine:~$
```

    b. Use lswh. This command displays the logical name of the connection and more details. However, you need admin permissions to run this command.

How do you run a command with elevated permissions in Ubuntu? How do you elevate to a superuser?

With the command **sudo**.

Let's give it a try. Type this command and press enter.

sudo -lshw -class network

```
jan@jan-virtual-machine:~$ sudo lshw -class network
[sudo] password for jan:
```

As you see now, it prompts for the password. By default, the person who installed the system becomes a superuser. However, on terminal, you always need to elevate, as it does not run by default in the superuser mode (although you can, it is better to avoid this practice).

```
*-network
       description: Ethernet interface
       product: 82545EM Gigabit Ethernet Controller (Copper)
       vendor: Intel Corporation
       physical id: 1
       bus info: pci@0000:02:01.0
       logical name: ens33
       version: 01
       serial: 00:0c:29:68:60:4d
       size: 1Gbit/s
       capacity: 1Gbit/s
       width: 64 bits
       clock: 66MHz
       capabilities: pm pcix bus_master cap_list rom ethernet physical logical t
p 10bt 10bt-fd 100bt 100bt-fd 1000bt-fd autonegotiation
       configuration: autonegotiation=on broadcast=yes driver=e1000 driverversio
n=7.3.21-k8-NAPI duplex=full ip=192.168.0.12 latency=0 link=yes mingnt=255 multi
cast=yes port=twisted pair speed=1Gbit/s
       resources: irq:19 memory:fd5c0000-fd5dffff memory:fdff0000-fdffffff iopor
t:2000(size=64) memory:fd500000-fd50ffff
```

    c.   If you want to view details of the ethernet networks (the wired network), use the command *ethtool*. Here I need to use the logical name of my ethernet which is ens33 in my case. You may need to install this if it does not exist.
        sudo ethtool ens33

3. Now let's configure our ethernet using commands. Let's add a static IP address.
    sudo ip addr add 192.168.0.200/24 dev ens33
    Here, dev stands for the device.
    This command will add an address, but it may add a secondary address if one address is already present.

4. To modify the address, let's use a new command *ifconfig*. First, let's install it. How do we install a package in Ubuntu? Using the **apt-get** command.
    sudo apt-get net-tools
    Once it is installed, you can use the following command.
    sudo ifconfig eth0 192.168.0.1 netmask 255.255.255.0
    To verify, run ifconfig command and press enter.

```
eth0      Link encap:Ethernet  HWaddr 00:0c:29:3c:73:32
          inet addr:192.168.0.1  Bcast:192.168.0.255  Mask:255.255.255.0
          inet6 addr: fe80::20c:29ff:fe3c:7332/64 Scope:Link
          UP BROADCAST RUNNING MULTICAST  MTU:1500  Metric:1
          RX packets:0 errors:0 dropped:0 overruns:0 frame:0
          TX packets:145 errors:0 dropped:0 overruns:0 carrier:0
          collisions:0 txqueuelen:1000
          RX bytes:0 (0.0 B)  TX bytes:31818 (31.8 KB)
```

You can also use the following command to verify the IP address.
ip address show dev dev_name
Replace the name with the name of your ethernet connection (e.g., ens33.
5. To set the link up and down, we will use the following commands.
    ip link set dev ens33 up
    ip link set dev ens33 down
6. To add a default gateway, use the command below.
    sudo ip route add default gw 192.168.0.10 eth0
7. To remove all the configuration,
    ip addr flush eth0
8. If you want to view the routing table, use *route -n* command. This is an example output of my routing table.

```
Kernel IP routing table
Destination     Gateway         Genmask         Flags Metric Ref    Use Iface
0.0.0.0         192.168.0.1     0.0.0.0         UG    0      0        0 eth0
10.10.10.0      0.0.0.0         255.255.255.0   U     1      0        0 eth0
```

Troubleshooting Installations

Sometimes, on rare occasions, you may receive the fatal error 11 (SIGSEGV). If an operating system installation accesses a memory location that is not supposed to, it will be stopped from proceeding further. SIGSEGV stands for Segment Violation Signal, in other words, a segmentation fault. This indicates a hardware related problem. If this was due to a problem in the hard disk, you can try wiping it and install again. If it is due to a memory fault, swapping memory modules wil work. You can also try disabling CPU cache in BIOS and see if it helps.

CHAPTER 3: Linux User Management

In this chapter you will learn

> sudo Command and Super/Root User
>
> Managing Users Through GUI/CLI
>
> Managing sudoers
>
> Command Aliases
>
> What is /ect/passwd
>
> Special Bits

In this chapter you will learn how to set up super user, how to modify the root user and other accounts, how to set up administrators, regular users and groups via the GUI, as well as from the command line.

sudo Command

Since you are new to the Linux operating system, you need to understand some basic commands in order to elevate yourself to the **su** or the super user.

sudo command elevates the users to the root user providing enough permissions to perform the administrative tasks. However, not everyone is going to get these permissions by default. The users must be added to the /etc/sudoers file in order to use this command.

Tip: If you want to handle the basics without being troubled by permission issues, you need to use the account of the user who installed the operating system. Or else you can switch to the root user. Both users are superusers.

Run this command and press enter in a terminal. If you want to switch to a user, use the su command (su – switch user). If you want to be placed in the home directory when you log in use su -

Tip: To access the terminal on Ubuntu, right click on Desktop and click *Open Terminal.*

Example: When you use Ubuntu first, you can take control of the **root** account. First, you need to set a password for the root and then proceed with switching the user.

```
jan@jan-virtual-machine:~$ su root
Password:
su: Authentication failure
jan@jan-virtual-machine:~$ sudo passwd root
Enter new UNIX password:
Retype new UNIX password:
passwd: password updated successfully
jan@jan-virtual-machine:~$ su root
Password:
root@jan-virtual-machine:/home/jan#
```

Yay! Now, you are the root user!

Adding Users to sudo Users List

To add a user to the sudo users list, you should use either the GUI or the *sudo visudo* command. Issue this command in a terminal.

Run the following command: *sudo visudo*

Image: sudo users list

Let's try to understand the file. There is the root user with root ALL=(ALL) ALL.

The first ALL means that the root user can use any terminal. The second means root can act as any user. Final ALL permits the user to run all the commands.

We can add more users with very specific control. For instance,

poweruser ALL= /sbin/poweroff command will allow the *poweruser* user to turn off the system via any terminal.

The next thing to learn is using the aliases. You can use several types of aliases in this file.

- Host_Alias
- User_Alias
- Runas_Alias
- Cmnd_Alias

For instance, the *sudoers* file may look like the following.

- Change the env_reset to env_reset,timestamp_timeout=n. Here you must replace n so that the session will not go any longer that the specified minutes. You can use -1 to stop the timeouts.
- By default, you do not see the password when you type when elevating to sudo. If you want to see the * when you type the password, use the pwfeedback to the above line. i.e., env_reset,pwfeedback.
- Create the alias and set permissions. See the example below.

```
Defaults      env_reset,pwfeedback,timestamp_timeout=15
Defaults      mail_badpass
Defaults
secure_path="/usr/local/sbin:/usr/local/bin:/usr/sbin:/usr/bin:/sbin:/bin:/snap/bin"

# Host alias specification
Host_Alias    LAN = jan.contoso.com, jake. contoso.com
Host_Alias    SRV = jan.host.com, drake.host.com, jake.host.com
Host_Alias    DNET = 10.1.2.0/255.255.255.0
# User alias specification
User_Alias    OPERATORS = dan
User_Alias    WEBADMIN = jan, sana
User_Alias    MAILADMIN = kane
# Cmnd alias specification
Cmnd_Alias    SU = /bin/su
Cmnd_Alias    HTTPD = /etc/rc.d/init.d/httpd, /etc/rc.d/init.d/mysql
# User privilege specification
root   ALL=(ALL:ALL) ALL
OPERATORS    ALL=ALL #The operators group has all the privileges.
jan2 DNET=(ALL)ALL
#jan2 has all the permissions through the DNET network.
# Members of the admin group may gain root privileges
%admin ALL=(ALL) ALL
print_operator ALL= PRINTING
#print_operator can run lpc and lprm from any computer.
# Allow members of group sudo to execute any command
%sudo  ALL=(ALL:ALL) ALL
```

> **Note**: If you are a first time Linux users, or a newbie, you may not understand the concepts at first. When you complete this lesson, you will gain a better understanding on how things work.

Adding a User through the GUI

Please follow these steps in order to add a user through Ubuntu GUI.

1. Open the Account Settings dialog, either through Ubuntu Dashboard ,or by clicking the down-arrow located at the upper right-hand corner on your Ubuntu screen.

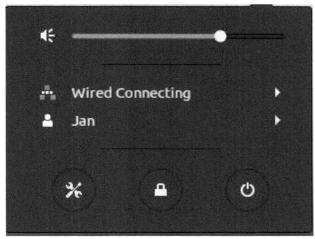

Image: Ubuntu user account

2. Next, click your username and then select Account Settings as follows.

Image: Ubuntu account settings

3. The following Users dialog will open.

Image: Ubuntu main user account

Note: All the fields will be disabled by default. You will need to provide authentication in order to move further passing this dialog.

4. Click the *Unlock* button located at the upper right-hand corner of the Users dialog. The following Authentication dialog will open for you to provide authentication information as an administrator because only this way you will be able to create or edit user accounts:

Image: Authentication request

5. Next, provide your password and then click the Authenticate button. You will now be able to see that all the fields in the *Users* dialog are enabled for you.
6. Click the Add User button. The Add User dialog will open for you to enter details of the new user you want to create.
7. You can specify if you want to create a Standard or an Administrative user through this dialog. It is also important to know that it is not a good security practice to leave the password field empty for the new user. This way any user can log in and access private and secure data on your system. Let's add *jake* as a new standard user.

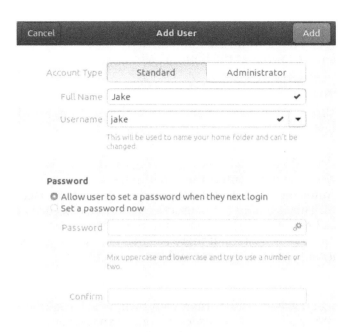

Image: Adding a new user

8. Click the Add button, which will only be enabled when you have provided all the valid information in the *Add User* dialog. The new user will now be created, and you will be able to see it in the Users dialog as follows:

Image: New standard user

9. You can also change the group to become an Administrator, select a locale, to reset the password, to enable automatic login, and to view the account activity.
10. To remove a user, you can use the remove button at the bottom right area.

Adding a User Through the Command Line

It is easier to manage users and groups through Linux command line. In this section, we will look into the techniques and examples.

User and Group Management in Linux

Linux is a multi-user platform. Most of the time in an enterprise environment or even in a SOHO environment, it is shared among multiple users. Some users and organizations used to share single account among several users. This is a dangerous practice in terms of security and availability. Therefore, the recommended best-practice is the creation of multiple accounts and distribute the permissions accordingly. In a Linux system, if there is a need for sharing files or directories, user and group management tools are more than capable.

Root or Superuser Privileges

Adding a new user involves administering an account other than your own, which requires superuser (AKA *root*) privileges. The same applies to other user or group management tasks, such as deleting an account, updating accounts, and creating and removing groups.

User managements tasks are the responsibility of the root user or the superuser as with any other operating system. This includes user as well as group management tasks. Since the account management requires security and safeguards, it is a must.

The user management tasks are carried out using the following commands.

- **su**: Switch user.

- **sudo**: Executes the commands with elevated privileges as the root user.

- **adduser**: Adds a user to a Linux system.

- **userdel**: Deletes a user account with or without user's files.

- **addgroup**: Adds a group.

- **delgroup**: Removes a group.

- **usermod**: This command can be used to modify users after adding.

- **chage**: This command can change the age of an account (change age). In other words, it is used to change the account expiry.

Files Involved

- **etc/passwd**: Holds user information.

- **ect/shadow**: Password encryption.

- **etc/sudoers**: Neither a user can perform administrative tasks nor provide administrative delegations if the user is not enlisted in this file. We have gone through the steps and modified this file in a recent section in this chapter.

- **etc/group**: This file holds all the group information.

Superuser is the all-powerful account with all the permissions to perform anything and everything. It is the alpha and omega. The root user can be configured after installing the operating system. By default, on Ubuntu, the system installer becomes a super user too. This isn't true for each and every Linux flavor.

How do we know if sudo is usable? Yes, it has to be installed and configured. Let's use the following command to verify it.

Command: *which sudo*

```
jan@jan-virtual-machine:~$ which sudo
/usr/bin/sudo
jan@jan-virtual-machine:~$
```

The command verifies and confirms the existence of sudo. If it does not on any occasion, use the following command to install it.

apt-get install sudo

Adding a New User Account

To get some hands-on experience, let's create a user named **Test2** using Ubuntu. It is always better if you change your user to the root user by using the *su-* command.

sudo adduser test2

Alternatively, switch to root first and then execute,

add user test2

```
root@jan-virtual-machine:/home/jan# sudo adduser test2
Adding user `test2' ...
Adding new group `test2' (1002) ...
Adding new user `test2' (1002) with group `test2' ...
Creating home directory `/home/test2' ...
Copying files from `/etc/skel' ...
Enter new UNIX password:
Retype new UNIX password:
passwd: password updated successfully
Changing the user information for test2
Enter the new value, or press ENTER for the default
        Full Name []: Testing Manager
        Room Number []:
        Work Phone []: 123-123-1234
        Home Phone []:
        Other []: Technical Support Manager
Is the information correct? [Y/n] Y
root@jan-virtual-machine:/home/jan#
```

You will be prompted to enter a password twice. Then it will be stored in the /etc/passwd file. In this file, colons are used as field separators. Upon creating users, it is possible to provide other information (e.g.full name). Some are optional (phone number, etc.).

When creating a user, a primary group is created using the same username of the user. The user is assigned to this group by default.

Sudoers - What is Is

The **sudoers** file was introduced earlier in this chapter. In order to delegate administrative tasks, it must be granted permission. This is achieved through adding newly created users to the **/etc/sudoers** file. In this section, the newly created user will be added to the sudoers file so that the user can be granted additional permissions to perform certain tasks.

1. Open /etc/sudoers file using *sudo visudo* command. In order to safeguard this file, do not open it using other editors. It is also better to use the root account by switching to it. It can make things secure and less painful. By opening this through visudo you ensure the following.
    a. Other users cannot edit the file simultaneously.
    b. The syntax is verified before exiting.
2. In the /etc/sudoers add a new entry for the new user account.

For instance, assume that you want you provide superuser permissions for **Test2**. To accomplish the task, add the following line at the bottom of **/etc/sudoers**:

test2 ALL=(ALL) ALL

```
# User privilege specification
root      ALL=(ALL:ALL) ALL
test2     All=(ALL:ALL) ALL
```

This line has the format **A B = (C:D) E**

This line has the format **A B = (C:D) E**

Let's refresh our memories about the content of this again.

- **A** represents the username.
- **B** represents the current host or all hosts in a networked environment.
- **C:D** represents the user and the group permissions. **Test2 is** allowed to run all commands as any user in any group. You must add **ALL:ALL** rather than **ALL**.
- **E** indicates the commands this user is allowed to execute. In this case, this user can run any command.
- The permission we granted is equivalent to the root account. It is advisable not to provide such permissions to users.

Creating Command Aliases

It is not advisable to directly provide the permissions to the users, as we did before. There is an alternative and more granular approach. For instance, it is possible to allow a set of commands and apply it to a user. We achieve this by grouping the commands into a set. This set is called an Alias.

In order to allow a helpdesk user to only use **adduser** and **usermod**, but no other commands, list the commands one by one (using **absolute paths**) at stated below. Assume we are providing the permission for an account named *helpdesk*. You can apply it to the *test2* or any other user you prefer.

- *helpdesk ALL=(ALL:ALL) /usr/sbin/adduser, /usr/sbin/usermod*

Alternatively, define an **alias** (which we can name as we wish as long as it's all upper case, for instance, **HELPDESK**)

Alternatively, as mentioned before, define an **alias**. We use uppercase letters to define aliases. This is how it is done.

- *Cmnd_Alias HELPDESK = /usr/sbin/adduser, /usr/sbin/usermod*

helpdesk ALL=(ALL:ALL) HELPDESK

```
# Cmnd alias specification
Cmnd_Alias HELPDESK = /usr/sbin/adduser, /usr/sbin/usermod
# User privilege specification
root    ALL=(ALL:ALL) ALL
helpdesk        All=(ALL:ALL) HELPDESK
```

Other than these specified here, *helpdek* will not be able to execute any other commands as root.

> **Note**: While saving, visudo will alert you if a syntax error is found in the file and indicate the line where the error is found at so that you can identify it more easily.
>
> **Tip**: For more information on the available options in /etc/sudoers, excute the command *man sudoers*.

Switching Users

Now that you have created the user and assigned permissions, and if the save was successful after editing the file, it is time to switch to this user and perform some tests. To do so, use the **su** command to switch to that account. As you now understand, you do not have to stick to a superuser account. You can switch back and forth instead. This will enforce security as well.

In addition, the -l option can be used to provide an environment like what the user would expect if he/she had directly logged in.

Execute the following command (example).

su- l helpdesk

More Advanced Commands

Let's learn the process of adding a new user. The theory will be important for the sake of administration. When a new user is added to the system, the following events and actions occur.

- His/her home directory is created (under */home* directory)
- The following files (hidden files) will be copies to the user's home directory. These are used to provide the required environment variables.
    - .bash_logout
    - .bash_profile
    - .bashrc
- Creating a mail spool at */var/spool/mail/username*.
- A group is created. The name of the group is same as the username.

Understanding the /etc/passwd

All the account information is stored in this file. A record exists per user in the following format.

[username]:[x]:[UID]:[GID]:[Comment]:[Home directory]:[Default shell]

- The username is the name of the user account.
- x means the account is protected by a shadow password in /etc/shadow
- UID and GID are User ID and Group ID.
- The Home directory points to the absolute (long) path to the user's home directory.

- The Default shell will be loaded when the user logs in.

Understanding the /etc/group

The group information is stored in /etc/group file. It has the following format.

[Group name]:[Group password]:[GID]:[Group members]

- Group name is the name of the group.
- Group password. If x is there, it is not used.
- GID is the same as in /etc/passwd
- Group members, a comma separated file.

Modifying a User

After adding a new user, his attributes can be modified using a special command known as **usermod**.

Syntax: *usermod [options] [username]*

Setting and expiry date example:

    usermod --expiredate 2020-01-31 helpdesk

Adding to multiple groups example:

    usermod --append --groups root,helpdesk helpdesk

Changing the home folder example:

    usermod --home /newhome/helpdesk helpdesk

Change the default shell example:

    usermod --shell /bin/sh helpdesk

```
jan@jan-virtual-machine:~$ groups jan
jan : jan adm cdrom sudo dip plugdev lpadmin sambashare
jan@jan-virtual-machine:~$ id jan
uid=1000(jan) gid=1000(jan) groups=1000(jan),4(adm),24(cdrom),27(sudo),30(dip),4
6(plugdev),116(lpadmin),126(sambashare)
jan@jan-virtual-machine:~$
```

We can use all the above examples together as follows.

usermod --expiredate 2020-01-31 --append --groups root,helpdesk --home /newhome/helpdesk helpdesk --shell /bin/sh helpdesk

Locking and Unlocking Users

It is possible to lock and unlock users. This is not helpful in regular operations, but very useful in work environments.

Lock example: *usermod --lock helpdesk*

Unlock example: *usermod --unlock helpdesk*

Group Management (Advanced)

Scenario: Let's assume that your company has a file sharing setup and you want to share a file to a group of users in HR department to read and write.

Commands:

- *groupadd hr_group*
- *chown :hr_group hr.txt*
- *usermod -aG hr_group user1*
- *usermod -aG hr_group user2*
- *usermod -aG hr_group user3*

Note: The **chwon** command is used to change the ownership of the user or a group. This is a new command that we will look into in more detail later. In this case, the file **hr** was changed and set the **hr_group**

If we take another example where 3 users need access to a file shared by one user, the grouping becomes very useful and secure. Let's assume there are 3 users,

- user1
- user2
- user3

The user1 has a file to be shared. If you change the file permission by issuing the command **chmod**. 660 means the owner and the group can read/write the file. However, if we use the default group created when the user1 is created, it will grant every other user in the same group to access all the files and personal data of user1. This is where the groups are important. You can set other groups and apply appropriate permissions. We can implement a proper grouping structure to better align the sharing and security.

Understanding the setuid, setgid, and Sticky Bit

This is a permission which can be applied to files, i.e., to an executable file. When you do so, the other users inherit the effective permissions from the owner. Therefore, it raises security concerns, and such applications must be kept to a minimum. This permission is used with the system programs.

For instance, let's take **usr/bin/passwd**. This is responsible for changing the password of a user. By doing so, it modifies the file **/etc/shadow**. For this file the superuser must be able to change his and other passwords, while the others must be able to change their own passwords but not any other's. Therefore, the rest of the users must be able to read and execute. To do so, the root must be able to specify accounts.

```
jan@jan-virtual-machine:/root$ ls -l /usr/bin/passwd
-rwsr-xr-x 1 root root 59640 Oct 23 00:35 /usr/bin/passwd
jan@jan-virtual-machine:/root$
```

Note the *rwsr* here. The **s** stands for the **setuid**. In this case, *setuid* and user's execute bit enabled ('s' means it is enabled, if it was 'S' instead, it means the execute bit is disabled).

When **setgid** bit is enabled, the effective GID of the real user becomes that of the group owner. Other users can access the file under the privilege of the group owner. If this is set on a directory the files created within this directory inherits the same group. New directories inherit the same *setgui*. When someone requires access to a shared directory, this is the best approach regardless the primary group of the file owner.

To enable the setgid, run the following command. Replace the filename with the name of the original file.

Command: *chmod g+s [filename]*

To send it in octal form (digits), you need to set the following. Replace the directory name from the name of your original directory.

Command: *chmod 2755 [directory]*

```
jan@jan-virtual-machine:~/Desktop$ chmod g+s test.txt
jan@jan-virtual-machine:~/Desktop$ chmod 2755 Test
Test/  Test1
jan@jan-virtual-machine:~/Desktop$ chmod 2755 Test/
jan@jan-virtual-machine:~/Desktop$ ls -l
total 20
lrwxrwxrwx 1 jan jan    5 ແ໐ 18 17:17 sym -> Test1
drwxr-sr-x 2 jan jan 4096 ແ໐ 18 17:17 Test
-rw-rw-r-- 1 jan jan   15 ແ໐ 18 17:15 Test1
-rw-rwSr-- 1 jan jan 1219 ແ໐ 18 17:47 test.txt
-rw-rw-r-- 1 jan jan   51 ແ໐ 18 18:02 testx.txt
-rw-r--r-- 1 jan jan   89 ແ໐ 18 18:03 testy
jan@jan-virtual-machine:~/Desktop$
```

Also note the color change of the test.txt file.

Tip: To undo, use -s. E.g., g-s

The Sticky Bit

If the sticky bit is enabled for **files**, it is **ignored** by the system. However, if it is set on a directory, it restricts users on actions, such as renaming and deleting, unless the user takes ownership, or becomes the root. To enable this bit, use one of the following commands below.

Command: *chmod o+t [directory]* or *chmod 1755 [directory]*

```
jan@jan-virtual-machine:~/Desktop$ chmod o+t Test/
jan@jan-virtual-machine:~/Desktop$ chmod o+t test.txt
jan@jan-virtual-machine:~/Desktop$ ls -l
total 20
lrwxrwxrwx 1 jan jan    5 ແ໐ 18 17:17 sym -> Test1
drwxr-xr-t 2 jan jan 4096 ແ໐ 18 17:17 Test
-rw-rw-r-- 1 jan jan   15 ແ໐ 18 17:15 Test1
-rw-rw-r-T 1 jan jan 1219 ແ໐ 18 17:47 test.txt
-rw-rw-r-- 1 jan jan   51 ແ໐ 18 18:02 testx.txt
-rw-r--r-- 1 jan jan   89 ແ໐ 18 18:03 testy
```

Also note the highlighted directory name in Blue.

Finally, there is even more granular permissions we can set with other commands, such as chattr, but we will look into these chapters in the next book in the series.

Deleting a Group

To delete a group, use the **groupdel** command.

Syntax: *groupdel [group_name]*

Example: *groupdel test2*

Deleting a User

To delete an account, use the **userdel** command.

Example: *sudo userdel test2*

CHAPTER 4: Linux Terminals, Editors and Shell

What you will learn in this chapter

 Terminal and Types

 Terminfo

 Console

 The Shell

 The Manual

 Editors

The Terminal

In the beginning of Unix and Linux, the computers those days didn't have graphical interfaces or environments. To interact with the operating system, there was a program called a terminal. It was mainly based on text. The early Linux versions also used an interface to let users interact with the operating system. It did not have advanced capabilities like now, or even graphical support. Therefore, it was called a **dumb terminal.** However, it provided a way to interact with the computer or remote computers. For security purposes, even now most servers run in text mode and interacted with graphical interfaces outside if required.

The terminal exists with Linux and now has advanced capabilities, such as block-mode graphics and vector graphics. It supports character sets such as:

- ASCII.
- ISO-8859-1, 2, 6, 7 and 8.
- ISO-10646 also known as Unicode.

Terminals support control codes for the control of features in the monitor and the keyboard. It also helps to control the cursor location and other non-printable operations. Some of the control codes include:

- Carriage return.
- Arrow keys.
- Page up/down.
- New line (line feed).

In addition, it used a display buffer to hold the history of commands. This was known as the *scroll region*. As the screen scrolls, the terminal was able to remember those data.

Tip: *To use old commands, use up arrow key in your keyboard.*

Another type of buffering is known as *alternate screen*. In this method, a terminal was able to store data in another screen instead of the monitor. This was the beginning of the simple graphics based on terminals. There was a control code to signal the terminal to switch the monitor between screen data and the alternate screen.

During the early days, there were special color-based text, such as bold and underline characters, blinking characters, and Black characters on White backgrounds. After a while, color terminals were available and there were multiple control codes to control the behaviors related to colors.

Today we are using advanced programs *emulating* those terminals. Such packages need special keys used by terminals those days. It is impractical for a keyboard to have a number of special keys to support terminals. Therefore, it is possible to map keys. However, mapping can be different from one system to another. There are some common keys available with most packages, such as the arrow keys, delete, repeat (sends the value of other keys), return (carriage return – similar to the enter key), break, and specific function keys (such as F1 to F12 in common keyboards).

The Terminfo

As you now understand, there are many terminal emulation packages emulating various terminals. For each terminal, the Linux operating system must keep the control codes so that it can distinguish and accurately operate the codes. These characteristics are in a place as a collection and it is called the *Terminfo database*.

To distinguish among the terminals, a folder is created to hold the set of files relating to that terminal. The folder is named after a character relating to the name of the terminal.

In Ubuntu, the terminfo location is /etc/terminfo/*/*

You can use the **toe** command to view all the available terminal types.

Example: *toe -a*

> ***Tip***: To learn more, use the terminal command *man terminfo* or visit
> http://manpages.ubuntu.com/manpages/xenial/man5/terminfo.5.html

The Console

In the early days, when you start a Linux machine, you just get a text-based console with a login prompt. You can authenticate and start sending commands. Modern Linux systems create several virtual consoles upon bootup. There can be up to 63 virtual consoles. You can switch between these consoles by using special key combinations or using the function keys of your keyboard. For instance, you could use Alt + Fn or Ctrl + Alt + Fn (here the simple n represents the number of a function key in your keyboard). In Ubuntu, you could open the text-based console by using Alt + Ctrl + F3. To get back, press Alt + Ctrl + F2.

```
Ubuntu 18.04.3 LTS jan-virtual-machine tty3

jan-virtual-machine login:
```

Image: The Ubuntu console

Types of Terminals

There are many types of terminals. We will look at a few popular and easy to us terminals.

xterm

This is the oldest X-Windows terminal emulation package available. This provides DEC VT 102/220 emulation CLI and Tektronix 4014 graphical environment.

Now there are emulators, such as Eterm and ROXterm, which are lightweight and offers great freedom of selecting features. While Eterm provides more flexibility, ROXterm offers features for power users. The following images shows the options available with xtem.

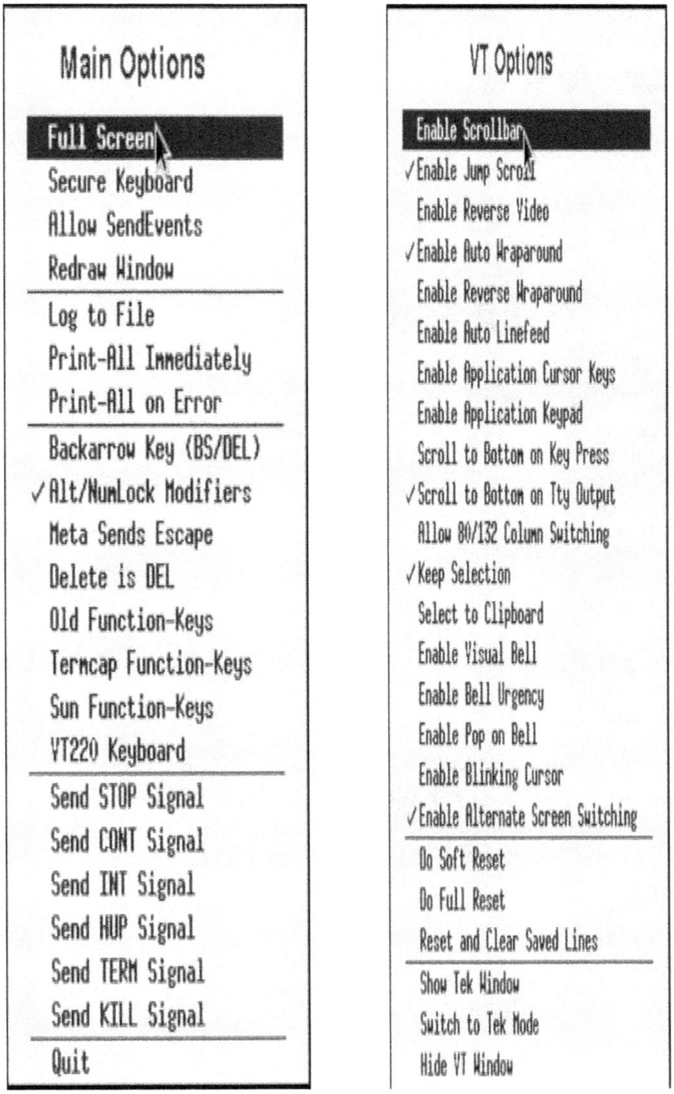

Image: xterm main and VT options

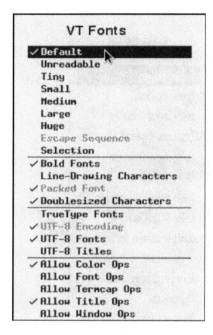

Image: VT fonts

Konsole

Konsole is the terminal emulator available with the KDE desktop environment. KDE has a menu bar similar to Windows and offers tabbed window sessions. These are convenient features of the Konsole. The most important feature of this is the **Profiles**. It offers saving and reusing settings of a tabbed session. It also offers a powerful bookmarking feature for directories and SSH. Other features include:

- Translucent background
- Split-view mode.
- Customizable color schemes and key-bindings.
- Incremental search.
- HTML compatible output.
- Terminal activity notifications.

For a set of command line options, please visit
https://docs.kde.org/stable5/en/applications/konsole/command-line-options.html

The GNOME terminal

GNOME also offers its own terminal emulator package the GNOME terminal. By default, Ubuntu comes with the GNOME terminal. It has lots of useful options. Let's find out which terminals exist with Ubuntu using a command.

Run the following command in the emulator.

update-alternatives --display x-terminal-emulator

GNOME terminal offers a rich set of features and commands. It supports tabs, attach/detach tabs, profiles, pre-determined sizes, etc.

There are new terminal emulators with cool features. Here is a list of those.

- **Xfce4**: For XFCE desktop environments.
- **Terminator** – https://launchpad.net/terminator
- **Tilda** - http://tilda.sourceforge.net/tildaabout.php
- **Guake** (Python-based): https://github.com/Guake/guake
- **Yakuake**: http://extragear.kde.org/apps/yakuake/
- **Eterm**: http://www.eterm.org/

Starting the Terminal in Ubuntu (GNOME)

To start the terminal, you can simply right click on the desktop or within a folder (an empty area). Terminal is also available in the docker at the left corner. You can also launch it from the Ubuntu software manager.

The Shell in a Nutshell

What is the shell? I introduced the shell in a previous chapter. Shell is the user interface and can be accessed through the terminal. Most of the time the default shell is the **bash** shell. Bash stands for **B**ourne **A**gain **SH**ell. The Bourne shell is the original Unix shell, and this is the Linux version of it. A shell provides interactive access to the operating system. There were other shells such as Dash (bash on Debian), ksh (Korn shell), zsh (Z shell) and csh (C shell).

The shell loads whenever you login, but it usually starts when you start the terminal program. If you log into a text-mode login, it loads as you log in. Depending on the user configuration, it loads appropriate features. We can see these configurations in /etc/passwd. For instance, for my account it is:

jan:x:1000:1000:Jan,,,:/home/jan:/bin/bash

As you can see at the end of the line, /bin/bash is the shell for this user.

Understanding the Shell Prompt

If you carefully look at the terminal you will see a bunch of text before a blinking cursor. This is the shell prompt. For me it is:

jan@jan-virtual-machine:~$

As you see, on Ubuntu the prompt uses a '$' sign. Some older systems might use '%' instead. C shell has '>'. Windows command prompt is similar to this if you are a Windows user. If a user elevates to root user (superuser) his prompt will change to a '#'.

From this point onward, we will be focusing on shell and it will be your companion for the rest of the course. It is quite useful, and it has many things to offer including help files, useful tips, etc.

Parts of the Prompt

- The username of the user who started the shell.
- Current virtual console.
- Current working directory (here ~ represents the home directory).

The default command prompt is controlled by an *environment variable* known as **PS1**. Another environment variable PS2 controls the next-tire command prompt. To display the current setting for you, try the following command.

echo $PS1

echo $PS2

```
jan@jan-virtual-machine:~$ echo $PS1
\[\e]0;\u@\h: \w\a\]${debian_chroot:+($debian_chroot)}\[\033[01;32m\]\u@\h\[\033
[00m\]:\[\033[01;34m\]\w\[\033[00m\]\$
jan@jan-virtual-machine:~$ echo $PS2
>
jan@jan-virtual-machine:~$ █
```

There are many characters controlling the bash shell prompt. Here is a list of characters.

Table: Bash shell character controls

Character	Description
\a	An ASCII bell character (07).
\d	The date in "Weekday Month Date" format.
\e	An ASCII escape character (033).
\h	The hostname up to the first `.'
\H	The hostname.
\j	The number of jobs currently managed by the shell.
\l	The base-name of the shell's terminal device.
\n	Newline.
\r	Carriage return.
\s	The name of the shell, the base-name of $
\t	The current time in 24-hour HH:MM:SS format.
\T	The current time in 12-hour HH:MM:SS format.
\@	The current time in 12-hour am/pm format.
\u	The username of the current user.
\v	The version of bash (e.g., 2.00).
\V	The release of bash, version + patchlevel (e.g., 2.00.0).
\w	The current working directory.
\W	Base-name of the current working directory.
\!	The history number of this command.
\#	The command number of this command.
\$	If the effective UID is 0, a #, otherwise a $
\nnn	The character corresponding to the octal number nnn.

\\	Backslash.
\[	Begins a sequence of non-printing characters, which could be used to embed a terminal control sequence into the prompt.
\]	End a sequence of non-printing characters.

Source: https://www.tldp.org/HOWTO/Bash-Prompt-HOWTO/bash-prompt-escape-sequences.html

You can customize your prompt using these characters in the following way.

```
jan@jan-virtual-machine:~$ PS1="\u@\h \t:\$ "
jan@jan-virtual-machine 18:47:36:$ PS1="\u@\h\w \t:\$ "
jan@jan-virtual-machine~ 18:48:30:$ PS1="\u@\h\W \t:\$ "
jan@jan-virtual-machine~ 18:48:57:$ PS1="\u@\h\$ "
jan@jan-virtual-machine$ PS1="\u@\h\w$ "
jan@jan-virtual-machine~$
```

Bash Color Codes

There are lots of customizations to the bash shell, such as font colors, background colors, effects such as blinking, bold, underline, and many more. For a great list of such please visit https://misc.flogisoft.com/bash/tip_colors_and_formatting

```
jan@jan-virtual-machine~$ PS1="\u@\h\w$ \e[92mLight green"
jan@jan-virtual-machine~$ Light green
jan@jan-virtual-machine~$ Light green
```

These customizations are not going to last for another session. To change these permanently, we will have to change the file associated with it. We will come to this point later.

The Man! The Manual

For any operating system, you get a manual available on the internet. For any GNU application this is the same. However, for bash there is a built-in manual and you must become familiar with it. It offers exceptional information and help when you do not know something, for instance, a new command.

The first command you are going to officially learn is **man**. As you are aware, no book can provide a more comprehensive guide on Linux commands and use with examples and practical use, but *man* can.

man Command Syntax, Output and Parameters

The following is the output of the command *man man*.

```
MAN(1)                        Manual pager utils                        MAN(1)

NAME
       man - an interface to the on-line reference manuals

SYNOPSIS
       man  [-C file]  [-d]  [-D]  [--warnings[=warnings]]  [-R encoding]  [-L
       locale] [-m system[,...]] [-M path] [-S list] [-e extension] [-i|-I]
       [--regex|--wildcard]   [--names-only]  [-a]  [-u]  [--no-subpages]  [-P
       pager] [-r prompt] [-7] [-E encoding] [--no-hyphenation] [--no-justifi-
       cation]  [-p  string]  [-t]  [-T[device]]  [-H[browser]]  [-X[dpi]]  [-Z]
       [[section] page[.section] ...] ...
       man -k [apropos options] regexp ...
       man -K [-w|-W] [-S list] [-i|-I] [--regex] [section] term ...
       man -f [whatis options] page ...
       man -l [-C file] [-d] [-D] [--warnings[=warnings]]  [-R  encoding]  [-L
       locale]  [-P  pager]  [-r  prompt]  [-7] [-E encoding] [-p string] [-t]
       [-T[device]] [-H[browser]] [-X[dpi]] [-Z] file ...
       man -w|-W [-C file] [-d] [-D] page ...
       man -c [-C file] [-d] [-D] page ...
       man [-?V]

DESCRIPTION
       man is the system's manual pager.  Each page argument given to  man  is
 Manual page man(1) line 1 (press h for help or q to quit)
```

Image: Linux man command

These manuals have several sections and you may want to save time by requesting the selection at once. The following list has the sections by numbers.

Table: Man page sections

Section	Content
1	User Commands
2	System Calls
3	Library Functions

4	Special Files (i.e., device files)
5	File Formats and File Systems
6	Games
7	Overview and Miscellaneous
8	System Administration and Privilege Commands
9	Kernel Routines
l	Local Documentation
n	New Pages

To get these definitions you can use the following command.

man n intro

Note: Replace n by a number/letter above.

```
INTRO(1)                    Linux User's Manual                    INTRO(1)

NAME
        intro - introduction to user commands

DESCRIPTION
        Section 1 of the manual describes user commands and tools, for example,
        file manipulation tools, shells, compilers, web browsers, file and image
        viewers and editors, and so on.

NOTES
        Linux is a flavor of UNIX, and as a first approximation all user com-
        mands under UNIX work precisely the same under Linux (and FreeBSD and
        lots of other UNIX-like systems).

        Under Linux, there are GUIs (graphical user interfaces), where you can
        point and click and drag, and hopefully get work done without first
        reading lots of documentation. The traditional UNIX environment is a
        CLI (command line interface), where you type commands to tell the com-
        puter what to do. That is faster and more powerful, but requires find-
        ing out what the commands are. Below a bare minimum, to get started.

    Login
        In order to start working, you probably first have to open a session by
Manual page intro(1) line 1 (press h for help or q to quit)
```

Image: A Linux man page

There is another important fact about these man pages. Each page has different sections. To reduce the time consumption, you have to have an idea of what these sections are.

Table: Parts of man page

Section	Purpose
Name	Name and a short description
Synopsis	Syntaxes
Description	A comprehensive description
Definitions	Program-related definitions
Examples	Examples
Overview	An outlook
Defaults	Defaults for the specific program/command
Options	Options for the specific program/command
Arguments	Possible arguments a user can supply
Parameters	Parameters storing values
Invocations	Specific related to invoking commands
Reserved Words	Reserved words for a system or a program
Exit Status	The exist status or code
Errors	Errors
Reporting Bugs	How to report bugs if found
Comments	Comments section

Environment	A set of environment variables used
Files	Related files, e.g., specific configuration files involved
Author	Author
Copyright	Copyright information
History	History of a program or a command
See Also	Related topics, e.g., commands

There are other sections, as well, and you can find even more if you are interested, by executing the *man bash* command or by visiting https://man.cx/bash#heading7

As you understand, there is a lot in a man page. Let's learn some more commands to shape the output.

man section_number page_name

Example: *man 4 tty*

```
TTY(4)                    Linux Programmer's Manual                    TTY(4)

NAME
       tty - controlling terminal

DESCRIPTION
       The file /dev/tty is a character file with major number 5 and minor num-
       ber 0, usually of mode 0666 and owner.group root.tty.  It is a  synonym
       for the controlling terminal of a process, if any.
```

Let's assume you want to find if a man page exists. *whatis* is the best command to find it. The syntax is,

whatis keyword

Example: *whatis*
man

```
jan@jan-virtual-machine:~$ whatis man
man (7)                    - macros to format man pages
man (1)                    - an interface to the on-line reference manuals
```

Now if you run *man 7 man* you will find more about macros.

```
MAN(7)                     Linux Programmer's Manual                     MAN(7)

NAME
       man - macros to format man pages

SYNOPSIS
       groff -Tascii -man file ...
```

If you do not know the specific page but you want to know about something specific such as shell for instance, or terminal, the following commands are helpful. The syntax is,

man – k keyword

Example: *man -k shell*

```
jan@jan-virtual-machine:~$ man -k shell
add-shell (8)          - add shells to the list of valid login shells
bash (1)               - GNU Bourne-Again SHell
capsh (1)              - capability shell wrapper
chroot (8)             - run command or interactive shell with special root direc...
chsh (1)               - change login shell
dash (1)               - command interpreter (shell)
dbus-launch (1)        - Utility to start a message bus from a shell script
envsubst (1)           - substitutes environment variables in shell format strings
flock (1)              - manage locks from shell scripts
gnome-shell (1)        - Graphical shell for the GNOME desktop
instmodsh (1)          - A shell to examine installed modules
pam_shells (8)         - PAM module to check for valid login shell
remove-shell (8)       - remove shells from the list of valid login shells
sh (1)                 - command interpreter (shell)
sh.distrib (1)         - command interpreter (shell)
shells (5)             - pathnames of valid login shells
systemd-debug-generator (8) - Generator for enabling a runtime debug shell and ...
whiptail (1)           - display dialog boxes from shell scripts
```

Now you can find the specific page,

man 1 dash for instance.

Less and More

These two commands are extremely helpful when using the man pages and even for other work, such as file operations.

These commands allow a user to read through a page or a file with lots of viewing options. Less is more advanced, and it loads fast because it does not load the entire file at once. It has many options than its cousin.

man is an old command and it is not friendly. For instance, you cannot scroll backward with it so reading becomes difficult. This led to the creation of its cousin *less*. *Less* provides a text editor like environment so that you can scroll back and forth, type arguments, and interact well. Let's take a look at the output of *man ls | more* command.

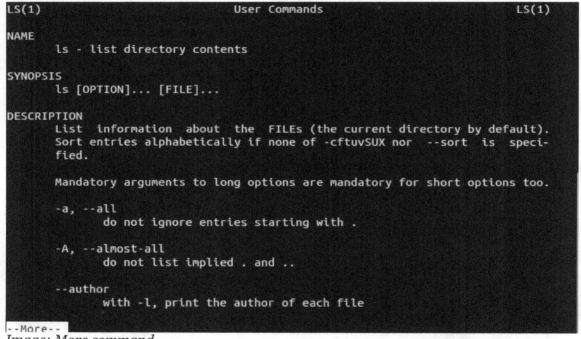

Image: More command

With more, you have to use either the enter key or the spacebar, not the arrow keys.

```
CAT(1)                          User Commands                          CAT(1)

NAME
       cat - concatenate files and print on the standard output

SYNOPSIS
       cat [OPTION]... [FILE]...

DESCRIPTION
       Concatenate FILE(s) to standard output.

       With no FILE, or when FILE is -, read standard input.

       -A, --show-all
              equivalent to -vET

       -b, --number-nonblank
              number nonempty output lines, overrides -n

       -e     equivalent to -vE

       -E, --show-ends
              display $ at end of each line
:
```

Image: Less command

There is a tiny ':' at the end. You can send commands to do additional operations. With less it is much easier to navigate and control.

You must have noticed the new symbol used with these commands.

To use these commands, you need to learn another new operator. This is known as **pipeline**.

A pipeline operator is simple and is '|'

What it does is, taking the result of a command and send it to another command, just like in a pipeline. For instance, let's look at the following example.

Syntax:

command_1 | command_2 | command_3 | .... | command_N

Example: *man bash | more*

The first command is executed first (*man bash* displays the manual for bash). Then it is piped to the second. This is a great way to chain commands.

Another example, ls /bin | more

```
bash
brltty
bunzip2
busybox
bzcat
bzcmp
bzdiff
bzegrep
:
```

In the next section, we are going to look at the commands in more structured way so the operations can be streamlined.

Linux Editors

There are lots of editors in the Linux world. If you are into scripting, you must have a working knowledge and be familiar with at least one editor. In this section, we will have a look at a few editors. As you already know, desktop environment releases have one editor of their own.

Vim Editor

In the old days, Unix systems used a text editor known as the vi editor. GNU made changes to this piece and made available as the "vi improved" or **vim**.

Vim editor is available in Cent OS or in Red Hat distributions. In Ubuntu, you may have to install it. There are some commands to verify if it exists. Issue, the following commands respectively.

alias vi

which vi

ls -l /usr/bin/vim

In ubuntu, you will get the following screen.

```
jan@jan-virtual-machine:/bin$ alias vi
bash: alias: vi: not found
jan@jan-virtual-machine:/bin$ which vi
/usr/bin/vi
jan@jan-virtual-machine:/bin$ ls -l /usr/bin/vi
lrwxrwxrwx 1 root root 20 ಅಕ್ಟೋ 17 04:21 /usr/bin/vi -> /etc/alternatives/vi
jan@jan-virtual-machine:/bin$
```

In this case, you must install vim by using the following command.

sudo apt-get install vim

When working with vim you must notice that there are two modes.

- Insert mode: press **i** key to get into the insert mode.
- Normal mode: press **Esc** to exit.

When you open a file with vim, you are in the normal mode. When you are in the insert mode, you are writing to the file. You must also know how to exit, save and exit.

- Press **q** to quit.
- Press **wq** to save to the same file and exit.
- Press **q!** to quit discarding changes.
- Type **w** *filename* to save the file in a different name.

Wim editor is a feature rich editor. It is not always convenient. For instance, it is not easy to copy paste. Yanking and visual modes will be utilized to do so.

Nano Editor

This tiny editor is available with most of the Linux systems, as well as Ubuntu.

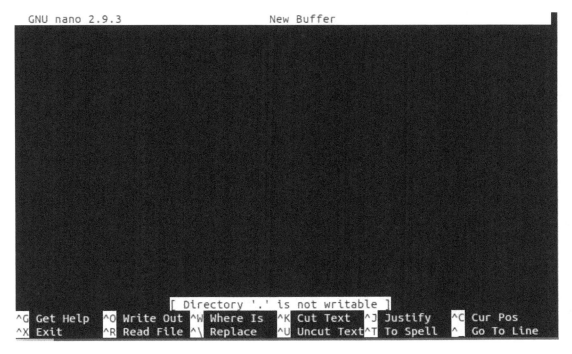

Image: Linux Nano editor

The best feature of this is the list of commands in front of the screen. It has a simple command set, the Ctrl key and another. To get help press Ctrl + G. To eixt, press Ctrl + X.

KDE Editors

With KDE, they ship editors and among the editors, **KWrite** and **Kate** are often used. While KWrite is a single editor, Kate is a multi-window and feature ich editor.

GNOME Editor

Since we are using Ubuntu, it is better to use a GNOME editor. gedit is the default editor in many cases.

Image: Linux Gnome editor

Gedit supports tabs, has a find and replace option, language, spelling, date/time tools, full screen mode, and a side panel. Another great feature is the printer support.

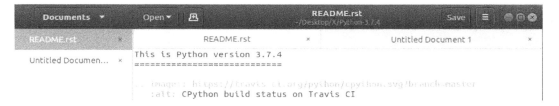

Image: Ubuntu gedit editor with the slide panel

CHAPTER 5: Basic Linux Shell Commands

In this chapter you will learn

Linux File System

Navigation

Listing Files with ls

/dev/null

Managing Directories, Files and Content

Hard and Soft Links

Introduction

We already explored commands in the previous chapters. We are not going to look at some useful commands for file handling and similar uses. Before going into more details, let's look at the Linux file structure.

Linux stores files in a structure known as the **virtual directory structure**. This is a single directory structure. It incorporates all the storage devices into a single tree. Each storage device is considered as a file. If you examine the path of a file, you do not see the disk information. For instance, the path to my desktop is, */home/jan/Desktop*. This does not display any disk information in its path. By this way, you do not need to know the underlying architecture.

If you are to add another disk to the existing, you simply use **mount point** directories to do so. Everything is connected to the root.

These files naming is based on the FHS (Filesystem Hierarchy Standard). Let's look at the common files once more. We already went through the directory types during the installation.

Table: Linux directory types

Directory	Purpose
/	This is the root home directory. The upper-most level.
/bin	This is the binary store. GNU utilities (user-level) exist in this directory.

/boot	This is where the system stores the boot directory and files used during the boot process.
/dev	Device directory and nodes.
/etc	This is where the system stores the configuration files.
/home	Home of user directories.
/lib	System and application libraries.
/media	This is where media is mounted, media such as CDs, USB drives.
/mnt	Where the removable media is mounted to.
/opt	Optional software packages are stored here.
/proc	Process information – not open for users.
/root	Home directory of root.
/run	Runtime data is stored here.
/sbin	System binary store. Administrative utilities are stored here.
/srv	Local services store their files here.
/sys	System hardware information is stored here.
/tmp	This is the place for temporary files.
/usr	This is where the user-installed software are stored.
/var	Variable director where the dynamic files such as logs are stored.

Tip: To clear the terminal use *clear* command.

Directory and File Navigation

To view a list of directories in the present directory, in Windows you use the *dir* command. This command works the same way on Linux.

To navigate to files, the most basic method is to use the full path to the file such as */home/jan/Desktop/*. There are basic commands to do this with easier.

1. Know your present working directory with *pwd* command.

```
jan@jan-virtual-machine:~/Desktop$ pwd
/home/jan/Desktop
jan@jan-virtual-machine:~/Desktop$
```

2. Change the directory location using the *cd* command. Here we use the **absolute path**.

```
jan@jan-virtual-machine:~/Desktop$ cd /usr/bin/
jan@jan-virtual-machine:/usr/bin$
```

3. Get back to the home directory using the cd command only.

```
jan@jan-virtual-machine:~/Desktop$ cd /usr/bin/
jan@jan-virtual-machine:/usr/bin$ cd
jan@jan-virtual-machine:~$ █
```

4. Now we will use the **relative path** to make things easier and less time-consuming. In this case, we can use the '/'.

```
jan@jan-virtual-machine:~$ dir
Desktop     Downloads          Music      Public      Videos
Documents   examples.desktop   Pictures   Templates
jan@jan-virtual-machine:~$ cd Desktop
jan@jan-virtual-machine:~/Desktop$ ▯
```

Here, the **dir** command lists directories under my current folder. I could jump to desktop folder using the command **cd Desktop**.

There are 2 special characters when it comes to directory traversal. Those are '.' And '..'. Single dot represents the current directory. Double dots represent the upper folder.

5. To go back to one level up, use the '..' for instance

```
jan@jan-virtual-machine:~/Desktop$ pwd
/home/jan/Desktop
jan@jan-virtual-machine:~/Desktop$ cd ..
jan@jan-virtual-machine:~$ █
```

6. You can also use '..' to skip typing folder paths. For instance,
7. You can go back one level and go forward. Here, you go up to the home folder and then go forward (down) to the Music folder.

```
jan@jan-virtual-machine:~$ cd Downloads
jan@jan-virtual-machine:~/Downloads$ cd ../Music
jan@jan-virtual-machine:~/Music$ ▮
```

8. You can do the '../' in a chain to go to a folder in an upper level, back and forth using absolute path (mixing relative and absolute paths).

```
jan@jan-virtual-machine:~/Music$ pwd
/home/jan/Music
jan@jan-virtual-machine:~/Music$ cd ../../../etc
jan@jan-virtual-machine:/etc$ cd /home/jan/Music
jan@jan-virtual-machine:~/Music$ cd ../../../etc/acpi
jan@jan-virtual-machine:/etc/acpi$ ▮
```

Listing Files

We use *ls* command to **list** files. This is one of the most popular commands among Linux users. Below is a list of ls commands and their use.

ls- a	List all files including all the hidden files starting with '.'
ls --color	Colored list [=always/never/auto]
ls -d	List the directories with '*/'
ls -F	Append indicator to entries (such as one of */=>@|)
ls -i	Lists the inode index
ls -l	List with long format including permissions
ls- la	Same as above with hidden files
ls -lh	The long list with human readable format
ls -ls	The long list with file size

ls -r	Long list in reverse
ls -R	List recursively (the directory tree)
ls -s	List file size
ls -S	List by size
ls -t	Sort by date/time
ls -X	Sort by extension name

Let's examine a few commands. Remember, you can use more than one argument. E.g., *ls -la*

Syntax: *ls [option ...] [file]...*

Detailed syntax:

ls [-a | --all] [-A | --almost-all] [--author] [-b | --escape]
  [--block-size=size] [-B | --ignore-backups] [-c] [-C] [--color[=when]]
  [-d | --directory] [-D | --dired] [-f] [-F | --classify] [--file-type]
  [--format=word] [--full-time] [-g] [--group-directories-first]
  [-G | --no-group] [-h | --human-readable] [--si]
  [-H | --dereference-command-line] [--dereference-command-line-symlink-to-dir] [--
hide=pattern] [--indicator-style=word] [-i | --inode]
  [-I | --ignore=pattern] [-k | --kibibytes] [-l] [-L | --dereference]
  [-m] [-n | --numeric-uid-gid] [-N | --literal] [-o]
  [-p | --indicator-style=slash] [-q | --hide-control-chars]
  [--show-control-chars] [-Q | --quote-name] [--quoting-style=word]
  [-r | --reverse] [-R | --recursive] [-s | --size] [-S] [--sort=word]
  [--time=word] [--time-style=style] [-t] [-T | --tabsize=cols]
  [-u] [-U] [-v] [-w | --width=cols] [-x] [-X] [-Z | --context] [-1]

Example: *ls -l setup.py*

```
jan@jan-virtual-machine:~/Desktop/X/terminator-1.91$ ls -l setup.py
-rwxrwxr-x 1 jan jan 8909 ☺♂  1  2017 setup.py
jan@jan-virtual-machine:~/Desktop/X/terminator-1.91$
```

This gives long list style details for this specific file.

More examples

List content of your home directory: *ls*

Lists content of your parent directory: *ls */*

Displays directories of the current directory: *ls -d */*

Lists the content of root: *ls /*

Lists the files with the following extensions: *ls *.{htm,sh,py}*

Lists the details of a file. If not found suppress the errors: *ls -myfile.txt 2>/dev/null*

A word on /dev/null

/dev/null is an important location. This is actually a special file called the **null device**. There are other names, such as **blackhole** or **bit-bucket**. When something is written to this file, it immediately discards it and returns and end-of-file (EOF).

When a process or a command returns an error STDERR or the standard error is the default file descriptor a process can write into. These errors will be displayed on screen. If someone wants to suppress it, that is where the null device becomes handy.

We often write this command line as /dev/null 2>&1. For instance,

ls- 0 > /dev/null 2>$1

What does it mean by 2 and $1. The file descriptors for Standard Input (stdin) is 0. For Standard Output (stdout), it is 1. For Standard Error (stderr) it is 2. Here, we are suppressing the error generated by the *ls* command. It is redirected to stdout and then writing it to the /dev/null thus discarding it immediately.

ls Color Codes

```
rs (reset to no color)
di (directory)
ln (symbolic link)
mh (multi-hardlink)
pi (named pipe, AKA FIFO)
so (socket) do (door)
bd (block device) cd (character device)
or (orphan symlink)
mi (missing file)
su (set-user-ID)
sg (set-group-ID)
ca (file with capability)
tw (sticky and other-writable directory)

st (sticky directory)
ex (executable file)
*.tar *.tgz *.arc *.arj *.taz *.lha *.lz4 *.lzh *.lzma *.tlz *.txz *.tzo *.t7z *
.zip *.z *.Z *.dz *.gz *.lrz *.lz *.lzo *.xz *.zst *.tzst *.bz2 *.bz *.tbz *.tbz
2 *.tz *.deb *.rpm *.jar *.war *.ear *.sar *.rar *.alz *.ace *.zoo *.cpio *.7z *
.rz *.cab *.wim *.swm *.dwm *.esd
*.jpg *.jpeg *.mjpg *.mjpeg *.gif *.bmp *.pbm *.pgm *.ppm *.tga *.xbm *.xpm *.ti
f *.tiff *.png *.svg *.svgz *.mng *.pcx *.mov *.mpg *.mpeg *.m2v *.mkv *.webm *.
ogm *.mp4 *.m4v *.mp4v *.vob *.qt *.nuv *.wmv *.asf *.rm *.rmvb *.flc *.avi *.fl
i *.flv *.gl *.dl *.xcf *.xwd *.yuv *.cgm *.emf *.ogv *.ogx
jan@jan-virtual-machine:~/Documents$ echo
```

Image: ls color codes

These color codes distinguish the file types quite well (you can find the script source at https://askubuntu.com/questions/17299/what-do-the-different-colors-mean-in-ls

Let's run *ls -lasSt*

```
jan@jan-virtual-machine:~/Documents$ ls -lasSth
total 16K
4.0K drwxr-xr-x  3 jan jan 4.0K ⬛⬛ 18 06:48 .
4.0K -rwxr-xr-x  1 jan jan 1.2K ⬛⬛ 18 06:47 ud.sh
4.0K drwxr-xr-x 16 jan jan 4.0K ⬛⬛ 17 21:30 ..
4.0K drwxrwxr-x  3 jan jan 4.0K ⬛⬛ 17 14:02 VMWare
```

This uses a long list format, displays all files, sorts by time. Now, you need to understand what these values are.

1. 4: File size (sorted by size).
2. In the next section d is for directory.
3. The next few characters represent permissions (r-read, w-write, x-execute).
4. Number of hard links.
5. File owner.
6. File owner's group.

7. Byte size.
8. Last modified time (sort by).
9. File/Directory name.

If you use **-i** in the command (S is removed, sorted by last modified time). You see the nodes in the left most area.

```
jan@jan-virtual-machine:~/Documents$ ls -lasthi
total 16K
 137988 4.0K drwxr-xr-x  3 jan jan 4.0K ಅಕ್ಟೋ 18 06:48 .
 146862 4.0K -rwxr-xr-x  1 jan jan 1.2K ಅಕ್ಟೋ 18 06:47 ud.sh
1184931 4.0K drwxr-xr-x 16 jan jan 4.0K ಅಕ್ಟೋ 17 21:30 ..
 139720 4.0K drwxrwxr-x  3 jan jan 4.0K ಅಕ್ಟೋ 17 14:02 VMWare
jan@jan-virtual-machine:~/Documents$
```

Example: ls -laxo

```
jan@jan-virtual-machine:~/Desktop/X/terminator-1.91$ ls -laxo
total 128
drwxrwxr-x 7 jan  4096 ಅಕ್ಟೋ  1  2017 .
drwxrwxr-x 4 jan  4096 ಅಕ್ಟೋ 17 16:59 ..
-rw-rw-r-- 1 jan   650 ಜೂನ್ 26  2017 AUTHORS
-rw-rw-r-- 1 jan 31703 ಜೂನ್ 26  2017 ChangeLog
-rw-rw-r-- 1 jan 17987 ಜೂನ್ 26  2017 COPYING
drwxrwxr-x 3 jan  4096 ಅಕ್ಟೋ  1  2017 data
drwxrwxr-x 2 jan  4096 ಅಕ್ಟೋ  1  2017 doc
-rw-rw-r-- 1 jan  1471 ಜೂನ್ 26  2017 INSTALL
-rw-rw-r-- 1 jan   281 ಅಕ್ಟೋ  1  2017 PKG-INFO
drwxrwxr-x 2 jan  4096 ಅಕ್ಟೋ  1  2017 po
-rw-rw-r-- 1 jan  2248 ಜೂನ್ 26  2017 README
-rwxrwxr-x 1 jan  3700 ಜೂನ್ 26  2017 remotinator
```

Using ls for Pattern Matching

The ls command can be used in conjunction with wildcards such as '*' and '?' Here the '*' represents multiple characters and '?' represents a single character.

In this example, we have the following folder with the following directories and files.

```
jan@jan-virtual-machine:~/Documents/VMWare/VMwareTools-10.3.10-12406962/vmware-t
ools-distrib$ dir
bin  caf  doc  etc  FILES  INSTALL  installer  lib  vgauth  vmware-install.pl
jan@jan-virtual-machine:~/Documents/VMWare/VMwareTools-10.3.10-12406962/vmware-t
```

We are trying to find a file with the name vm* (vm and any characters to the right). And then we will try to match the INSTALL name of the file. In the first attempt it fails as there 4 '?'s. The next one succeeds.

```
jan@jan-virtual-machine:~/Documents/VMWare/VMwareTools-10.3.10-12406962/vmware-t
ools-distrib$ ls -l vm*
-rwxr-xr-x 1 jan jan 227024 ౦ఌ 20  2019 vmware-install.pl
jan@jan-virtual-machine:~/Documents/VMWare/VMwareTools-10.3.10-12406962/vmware-t
ools-distrib$ ls -l IN????
ls: cannot access 'IN????': No such file or directory
jan@jan-virtual-machine:~/Documents/VMWare/VMwareTools-10.3.10-12406962/vmware-t
ools-distrib$ ls -l IN?????
-rw-r--r-- 1 jan jan 2538 ౦ఌ 20  2019 INSTALL
jan@jan-virtual-machine:~/Documents/VMWare/VMwareTools-10.3.10-12406962/vmware-t
ools-distrib$ █
```

We will now use the **or** logic to match a pattern.

Image: Folders in my directory

Let's see if we can only list the directories with the characters **a** and **i** in the middle.

```
jan@jan-virtual-machine:~/Desktop/Y$ ls -l sn[ai]pt
snapt:
total 0

snipt:
total 0
jan@jan-virtual-machine:~/Desktop/Y$ █
```

Another example using pipes:

ls -la | less

```
total 1080
drwxr-xr-x 18 jan jan   4096 ထထၖ   17 17:05 .
drwxrwxr-x  4 jan jan   4096 ထထၖ   17 16:59 ..
-rw-r--r--  1 jan jan  10953 ႕ၖ     8 23:33 aclocal.m4
drwxr-xr-x  2 jan jan   4096 ႕ၖ     8 23:33 .azure-pipelines
-rw-r--r--  1 jan jan    631 ႕ၖ     8 23:33 CODE_OF_CONDUCT.rst
-rwxr-xr-x  1 jan jan  44166 ႕ၖ     8 23:33 config.guess
-rw-r--r--  1 jan jan   6507 ထထၖ   17 17:05 config.log
-rwxr-xr-x  1 jan jan  36251 ႕ၖ     8 23:33 config.sub
:
```

Handling Files

In this section, we will create, modify, copy, move and delete files. You will also learn how to read files and do other tasks.

Creating a File

To create files and to do some more tasks we use the command **touch**.

touch test.txt

```
jan@jan-virtual-machine:~/Desktop$ touch test1.txt
jan@jan-virtual-machine:~/Desktop$ ls
test1.txt  X  Y
jan@jan-virtual-machine:~/Desktop$
```

Syntax: *touch [OPTION]... FILE...*

Detailed syntax: *touch [[-a] [-m] | [--time=timetype] [...]] [[-d datestring] | [-t timestamp]] [-c] [-f] [-h] [-r reffile] file [file ...]*

This command can also be used to change the **file access time** of a file.

```
jan@jan-virtual-machine:~/Desktop$ ls -l test1.txt
-rw-r--r-- 1 jan jan 0 ထထၖ 18 10:27 test1.txt
jan@jan-virtual-machine:~/Desktop$ touch test1.txt
jan@jan-virtual-machine:~/Desktop$ ls -l test1.txt
-rw-r--r-- 1 jan jan 0 ထထၖ 18 10:35 test1.txt
jan@jan-virtual-machine:~/Desktop$
```

To change only the last access time, use *-a*.

Example: *touch -a test1.txt*

```
jan@jan-virtual-machine:~/Desktop$ ls -l test1.txt
-rw-r--r-- 1 jan jan 0 coo 18 10:35 test1.txt
jan@jan-virtual-machine:~/Desktop$ touch -a test1.txt
jan@jan-virtual-machine:~/Desktop$ ls -l test1.txt
-rw-r--r-- 1 jan jan 0 coo 18 10:35 test1.txt
jan@jan-virtual-machine:~/Desktop$ ls -l --time=atime test1.txt
-rw-r--r-- 1 jan jan 0 coo 18 10:39 test1.txt
jan@jan-virtual-machine:~/Desktop$
```

Here, to view the output you use *–time* parameter in the ls command. With only the ls -l it does not display the *last access time* but the *last modified time*.

Copying Files

To copy files, use the **cp** command.
Syntax: *cp [option]... [-T] source destination*

Example: *cp test1.txt test2.txt*

```
jan@jan-virtual-machine:~/Desktop$ cp test1.txt test2.txt
jan@jan-virtual-machine:~/Desktop$ ls -l test*
-rw-r--r-- 1 jan jan 12 coo 18 10:45 test1.txt
-rw-r--r-- 1 jan jan 12 coo 18 10:46 test2.txt
jan@jan-virtual-machine:~/Desktop$
```

Copy command can be dangerous as it does not ask if test2.txt exists. It leads to a data loss. Therefore, always use **-i** option.

```
jan@jan-virtual-machine:~/Desktop$ cp -i test1.txt test2.txt
cp: overwrite 'test2.txt'?
```

You can answer with *y* or *n* to accept or deny.

Copying a file to another directory: *cp test1.txt /home/jan/Documents*

```
jan@jan-virtual-machine:~/Desktop$ cp test1.txt /home/jan/Documents
jan@jan-virtual-machine:~/Desktop$
```

Using relative path instead the absolute path.

Now I am at the following directory: */home/jan/Desktop*. I want to copy a file to
/home/jan/Documents
Command: *cp test1.txt ../Documents*

```
jan@jan-virtual-machine:~/Desktop$ cp test1.txt ../Documents/
jan@jan-virtual-machine:~/Desktop$ ▮
```

Copy a file to the present working directory using the relative path. Here we will use '.' to
denote the pwd.

```
jan@jan-virtual-machine:~/Desktop$ pwd
/home/jan/Desktop
jan@jan-virtual-machine:~/Desktop$ ls
test1.txt   test2.txt   X   Y
jan@jan-virtual-machine:~/Desktop$ cp /bin/bash .
jan@jan-virtual-machine:~/Desktop$ ls
bash    test1.txt    test2.txt   X   Y
jan@jan-virtual-machine:~/Desktop$
```

Recursively copy files and folders

Example: cp -R copies the folder snapt with files to
snipt.

```
jan@jan-virtual-machine:~/Desktop$ ls ./Y/snapt
test1.txt   test2.txt
jan@jan-virtual-machine:~/Desktop$ ls ./Y
snapt   snipt   snopt
jan@jan-virtual-machine:~/Desktop$ cp -R ./Y/snapt ./Y/snipt
jan@jan-virtual-machine:~/Desktop$
```

Let's copy a set of files recursively from one directory to its sub directory.
Command: *cp -R ./Y/snapt/test* ./Y/snopt*

```
jan@jan-virtual-machine:~/Desktop$ ls ./Y
snapt   snipt   snopt   test1.txt   test2.txt
```

This is my desktop. I have these files in the Y directory on Desktop. I want to copy test1.txt and
test2.txt from Y to snopt directory. After executing the command,

```
jan@jan-virtual-machine:~/Desktop$ ls -l ./Y/snopt/
total 8
-rw-r--r-- 1 jan jan 12 ಚಿ:ಇ 18 11:24 test1.txt
-rw-r--r-- 1 jan jan 12 ಚಿ:ಇ 18 11:24 test2.txt
jan@jan-virtual-machine:~/Desktop$ ▮
```

How to use wildcards? We already used it in this example, haven't we?

Tip: If the file names are long, use the Tab key to autocomplete the file name(s). In any operation Tab key automatically fills the file/directory names

Linking Files with Hard and Symbolic Links

Another feature of the Linux file system is the ability to link files. Without maintaining original copies of files everywhere, you can link files to keep virtual copies of the same file. You can think of a link as a placeholder. There are 2 types of links,
- Symbolic links
- Hard links

A symbolic link is another physical file. It is not a shortcut. This file is linked to another file in the file system. Unlike a shortcut, the symlink gets instant access to the data object.

Syntax: ln -s [OPTIONS] FILE LINK

Example: ln -s ./Y/test1.txt testn.txt

```
jan@jan-virtual-machine:~/Desktop$ ln -s ./Y/test1.txt testn.txt
jan@jan-virtual-machine:~/Desktop$ ls -l
total 1096
-rwxr-xr-x 1 jan jan 1113504 ಚಿ:ಇ 18 11:07 bash
lrwxrwxrwx 1 jan jan      13 ಚಿ:ಇ 18 12:24 testn.txt -> ./Y/test1.txt
drwxrwxr-x 4 jan jan    4096 ಚಿ:ಇ 17 16:59 X
drwxr-xr-x 5 jan jan    4096 ಚಿ:ಇ 18 11:22 Y
jan@jan-virtual-machine:~/Desktop$ ▮
```

If you check the inode you will see these are different files. The size can tell the same difference.
- 279185 test1.txt
- 1201056 testn.txt

When you create symlinks, the destination file should not be there (especially directory with the destination symlink name should not be there). However, you can force the command to create or replace the file.

```
jan@jan-virtual-machine:~/Desktop$ ln -s ./Y/test1.txt .
ln: failed to create symbolic link './test1.txt': File exists
jan@jan-virtual-machine:~/Desktop$ ln -sf ./Y/test1.txt .
jan@jan-virtual-machine:~/Desktop$ █
```

The ln command is also valid for directories.

```
drwxrwxr-x 2 jan jan    4096 ឧ:ឌ  18 12:44 B
-rwxr-xr-x 1 jan jan 1113504 ឧ:ឌ  18 11:07 bash
lrwxrwxrwx 1 jan jan       1 ឧ:ឌ  18 13:54 T -> X        ⬅
lrwxrwxrwx 1 jan jan      13 ឧ:ឌ  18 12:24 testn.txt -> ./Y/test1.txt
drwxrwxr-x 4 jan jan    4096 ឧ:ឌ  18 13:57 X
drwxr-xr-x 5 jan jan    4096 ឧ:ឌ  18 12:45 Y
```

If you wish to overwrite symlinks, you have to use the -f as stated above. Or else, if you want to replace the symlink from a file to another, use **-n**.

Example: I have 2 directories dir1 and dir2 on my desktop. I create a symlink - dir1 to sym. Then I want to link sym to dir 2 instead. If I use -s and -f together (-sf) it does not work. The option to us here is **-n**.

```
jan@jan-virtual-machine:~/Desktop$ ls
bash  dir1  dir2  test1.txt  test2.txt  X  Y
jan@jan-virtual-machine:~/Desktop$ ln -s dir1 sym
jan@jan-virtual-machine:~/Desktop$ ls -l
total 1104
-rwxr-xr-x 1 jan jan 1113504 ੪੪ 18 11:07 bash
drwxr-xr-x 2 jan jan    4096 ੪੪ 18 14:31 dir1
drwxr-xr-x 2 jan jan    4096 ੪੪ 18 14:31 dir2
lrwxrwxrwx 1 jan jan       4 ੪੪ 18 14:34 sym -> dir1
lrwxrwxrwx 1 jan jan      13 ੪੪ 18 14:17 test1.txt -> ./Y/test1.txt
lrwxrwxrwx 1 jan jan      13 ੪੪ 18 14:14 test2.txt -> ./Y/test2.txt
drwxrwxr-x 4 jan jan    4096 ੪੪ 18 14:00 X
drwxr-xr-x 5 jan jan    4096 ੪੪ 18 12:45 Y
jan@jan-virtual-machine:~/Desktop$ ln -s dir2 sym
jan@jan-virtual-machine:~/Desktop$ ls -l
total 1104
-rwxr-xr-x 1 jan jan 1113504 ੪੪ 18 11:07 bash
drwxr-xr-x 2 jan jan    4096 ੪੪ 18 14:35 dir1
drwxr-xr-x 2 jan jan    4096 ੪੪ 18 14:31 dir2
lrwxrwxrwx 1 jan jan       4 ੪੪ 18 14:34 sym -> dir1
lrwxrwxrwx 1 jan jan      13 ੪੪ 18 14:17 test1.txt -> ./Y/test1.txt
lrwxrwxrwx 1 jan jan      13 ੪੪ 18 14:14 test2.txt -> ./Y/test2.txt
drwxrwxr-x 4 jan jan    4096 ੪੪ 18 14:00 X
drwxr-xr-x 5 jan jan    4096 ੪੪ 18 12:45 Y
jan@jan-virtual-machine:~/Desktop$ ln -sf dir2 sym
jan@jan-virtual-machine:~/Desktop$ ls -l
total 1104
-rwxr-xr-x 1 jan jan 1113504 ੪੪ 18 11:07 bash
drwxr-xr-x 2 jan jan    4096 ੪੪ 18 14:35 dir1
drwxr-xr-x 2 jan jan    4096 ੪੪ 18 14:31 dir2
lrwxrwxrwx 1 jan jan       4 ੪੪ 18 14:34 sym -> dir1
lrwxrwxrwx 1 jan jan      13 ੪੪ 18 14:17 test1.txt -> ./Y/test1.txt
lrwxrwxrwx 1 jan jan      13 ੪੪ 18 14:14 test2.txt -> ./Y/test2.txt
drwxrwxr-x 4 jan jan    4096 ੪੪ 18 14:00 X
drwxr-xr-x 5 jan jan    4096 ੪੪ 18 12:45 Y
jan@jan-virtual-machine:~/Desktop$ ln -sfn dir2 sym
jan@jan-virtual-machine:~/Desktop$ ls -l
total 1104
-rwxr-xr-x 1 jan jan 1113504 ੪੪ 18 11:07 bash
drwxr-xr-x 2 jan jan    4096 ੪੪ 18 14:35 dir1
drwxr-xr-x 2 jan jan    4096 ੪੪ 18 14:31 dir2
lrwxrwxrwx 1 jan jan       4 ੪੪ 18 14:35 sym -> dir2
lrwxrwxrwx 1 jan jan      13 ੪੪ 18 14:17 test1.txt -> ./Y/test1.txt
lrwxrwxrwx 1 jan jan      13 ੪੪ 18 14:14 test2.txt -> ./Y/test2.txt
drwxrwxr-x 4 jan jan    4096 ੪੪ 18 14:00 X
drwxr-xr-x 5 jan jan    4096 ੪੪ 18 12:45 Y
jan@jan-virtual-machine:~/Desktop$ ▮
```

Unlinking

To remove the symlinks you can use the following commands.
- **Syntax**: *unlink linkname*
- **Syntax**: *rm linkname*

Creating Hard Links

Now we will look at creating hard links. Hard link creates a separate virtual file. This file includes information about the original file and its location.

Example: *ln test1.txt hard_link*

```
jan@jan-virtual-machine:~/Desktop$ ln test1.txt hard_link
jan@jan-virtual-machine:~/Desktop$ ls -l
```

```
jan@jan-virtual-machine:~/Desktop$ ls -l --block-size=M
total 1M
-rw-r--r-- 2 jan jan 1M ಅಕ್ಟೋ 18 10:45 hard_link
-rw-r--r-- 2 jan jan 1M ಅಕ್ಟೋ 18 10:45 test1.txt
drwxrwxr-x 4 jan jan 1M ಅಕ್ಟೋ 18 14:00 X
drwxr-xr-x 5 jan jan 1M ಅಕ್ಟೋ 18 12:45 Y
jan@jan-virtual-machine:~/Desktop$ ^C
jan@jan-virtual-machine:~/Desktop$
```

Here we do not see any symbolic representations. That means the file is an actual physical file. And if you look at the **inode**, you will see both files having the same inode number.

```
jan@jan-virtual-machine:~/Desktop$ ls -li
total 16
1201056 -rw-r--r-- 2 jan jan   12 ಅಕ್ಟೋ 18 10:45 hard_link
1201056 -rw-r--r-- 2 jan jan   12 ಅಕ್ಟೋ 18 10:45 test1.txt
1183761 drwxrwxr-x 4 jan jan 4096 ಅಕ್ಟೋ 18 14:00 X
 279178 drwxr-xr-x 5 jan jan 4096 ಅಕ್ಟೋ 18 12:45 Y
```

How do we identify a hard link? Usually the files connected to a file is 1. In other words, itself. If the number is 2, that means it has a connection to another file.
Another example,

```
jan@jan-virtual-machine:~/Desktop$ ls -lt LICENSE
-rw-r--r-- 1 jan jan 12769 ಅಕ್ಟೋ  8 23:33 LICENSE
jan@jan-virtual-machine:~/Desktop$ ln LICENSE LIC_HARD
jan@jan-virtual-machine:~/Desktop$ ls -lt LICENSE
-rw-r--r-- 2 jan jan 12769 ಅಕ್ಟೋ  8 23:33 LICENSE
jan@jan-virtual-machine:~/Desktop$ ls -lt LIC_HARD
-rw-r--r-- 2 jan jan 12769 ಅಕ್ಟೋ  8 23:33 LIC_HARD
jan@jan-virtual-machine:~/Desktop$
```

Symbolic link does not change this increment of hard link number for each file. See the following example.

```
jan@jan-virtual-machine:~/Desktop$ ls -lt *LIC*
lrwxrwxrwx 1 jan jan      7 ಐ 18 15:57 SymLIC -> LICENSE
-rw-r--r-- 1 jan jan 12769 ಐ  8 23:33 LICENSE
```

What happens if the original file is removed?

```
jan@jan-virtual-machine:~/Desktop$ ls -lt
total 12
lrwxrwxrwx 1 jan jan    9 ಐ 18 15:46 sym -> test1.txt
drwxrwxr-x 4 jan jan 4096 ಐ 18 14:00 X
drwxr-xr-x 5 jan jan 4096 ಐ 18 12:45 Y
-rw-r--r-- 1 jan jan   12 ಐ 18 10:45 hard_link
```

Now here you can see the hard_link has reduced to its links to 1. The symbolic link displays a broken or what we call the **orphan** state.

> **Tip**: Another question would be if a hard link can connect to symbolic links and can symbolic links can have another symbolic links. The answer is yes.

File Renaming

Next, we will look at how file renaming works. For this the command used is **mv**. mv stands for "move".

Syntax: *mv [options] source dest*

Example: *mv LICENSE LICENSE_1*

You must be cautious when you use this command. If you do the following, what would happen?

> **Scenario**: I have a test1.txt file and a test2.txt file on my desktop. I want to rename the text1.txt to text2.txt. If we use the *mv text1.txt to text2.txt* the text2.txt file **will be replaced** by the text1.txt! Therefore, you should not use this command when there is another file with the same name.

One advantage of this command is that you can move and rename the file all together, especially when you do it from one location to another.

Example: Moving /home/jan/Desktop/Y/snapt to /Desktop while renaming it so Snap. This is similar to a cut and paste on Windows except for the renaming part.
Example: *mv /home/jan/Desktop/Y/snapt/ ./Snap*

> ***Tip***: Can you use wildcards with the *mv* command? Yes! You can even perform bulk operations.

```
jan@jan-virtual-machine:~/Desktop$ ls
Temp  test  test1.txt  test2  test2.txt
jan@jan-virtual-machine:~/Desktop$ mv test* Temp/
jan@jan-virtual-machine:~/Desktop$ █
```

Removing Files

To remove files, use **rm** command. rm command does not ask you if you want to delete the file. Therefore, you must use the **-i** option with it.

Syntax: *rm [OPTION]... FILE...*

Managing Directories

There is a set of commands to create and remove directories.
- To create a directory, use the **mkdir** command.
- To remove a directory, use the **rmdir** command.

Syntax: *mkdir [-m=mode] [-p] [-v] [-Z=context] directory [directory ...]*
  rmdir [-p] [-v | –verbose] [–ignore-fail-on-non-empty] [directories ...]

Example: Creating a set of directories with the *mkdir* command. To create a tree of directories you must use -p. If you try without it, you won't succeed.
```
jan@jan-virtual-machine:~/Desktop$ mkdir ./Dir1/Dir1_Child1/Child1_Child2
mkdir: cannot create directory './Dir1/Dir1_Child1/Child1_Child2': No such file
or directory
```

Command: *mkdir -p ./Dir1/Dir1_Child1/Child1_Child2*
```
jan@jan-virtual-machine:~/Desktop$ mkdir -p ./Dir1/Dir1_Child1/Child1_Child2
```

Example: *rmdir ./Dir1/Dir1_Child1/Child1_Child2*

> ***Note***: This only removes the Child1_Child2 folder. Not the entire directory.

To remove a directory with the *rmdir* command is not possible if the directory has files in it.

```
jan@jan-virtual-machine:~/Desktop/Temp$ ls
test  test1.txt  test2  test2.txt
jan@jan-virtual-machine:~/Desktop/Temp$ cd ..
jan@jan-virtual-machine:~/Desktop$ rmdir Temp/
rmdir: failed to remove 'Temp/': Directory not empty
```

You have to remove the files first in order to remove the directory. In this case, you can use another command to do this recursively.

Example: *rm -rf /Temp*

```
jan@jan-virtual-machine:~/Desktop$ rm -rf Temp/
jan@jan-virtual-machine:~/Desktop$ 
```

Caution: This is an extremely dangerous command! When you exercise it, you must be extremely cautious as it does not prompt you for permissions.

Managing File Content

File content management is extremely useful for day to day work. You can use several commands to view and manage content.

Let's look at the **file** command first. It helps us to have a peak into the file and see what it actually is. It can do more.
- This command provides an overview of the file.
- It tells you if the file is a directory.
- It tells you if the file is a symbolic link.
- It can display file properties especially against binary executables (a secure operation).
- It may brief you about the content (i.e., when executed against a script file).

Syntax: *file [option] [filename]*

```
jan@jan-virtual-machine:~/Desktop$ file Test1
Test1: ASCII text
jan@jan-virtual-machine:~/Desktop$ file Test
Test: directory
jan@jan-virtual-machine:~/Desktop$ file sym
sym: symbolic link to Test1
jan@jan-virtual-machine:~/Desktop$ ln Test1 Test_HL
jan@jan-virtual-machine:~/Desktop$ file Test_HL
Test_HL: ASCII text
jan@jan-virtual-machine:~/Desktop$ file /bin/busybox
/bin/busybox: ELF 64-bit LSB executable, x86-64, version 1 (GNU/Linux), statical
ly linked, for GNU/Linux 3.2.0, BuildID[sha1]=4da2c17557aa874a0ddb321eb9dd6fd121
8d3145, stripped
jan@jan-virtual-machine:~/Desktop$ file /sbin/acpi_available
/sbin/acpi_available: POSIX shell script, ASCII text executable
jan@jan-virtual-machine:~/Desktop$ █
```

Note: As you see it does not show anything about a hard link.

Viewing Files with cat Command

To view files, you cannot use the file command. You can use a more versatile command known as **cat**.

Syntax: *cat [OPTION] [FILE]...*

This command is an excellent tool to view a certain file or files at once, parts of the files and especially logs.

Example: *cat test.txt*

```
jan@jan-virtual-machine:~/Desktop$ cat test.txt
    1. This is a test 1
    2. This is a test 1
    3. This is a test 1
    4. This is a test 1
    5. This is a test 1
    6. This is a test 1
    7. This is a test 1
    8. This is a test 1
    9. This is a test 1
    10. This is a test 1
    11. This is a test 1
    12. This is a test 1
    13. This is a test 1
    14. This is a test 1
    15. This is a test 1
```

Example: Viewing 2 files together.
Command: cat test.txt testx.txt

```
jan@jan-virtual-machine:~/Desktop$ cat test.txt testx.txt
    1. This is a test 1
    2. This is a test 1
    3. This is a test 1
    4. This is a test 1
    5. This is a test 1
    6. This is a test 1
    7. This is a test 1
    8. This is a test 1
    9. This is a test 1
    10. This is a test 1
    11. This is a test 1
    12. This is a test 1
    13. This is a test 1
    14. This is a test 1
    15. This is a test 1
    1. This is a test 1
    2. This is a test 1
```

Creating files with cat is also possible. The following command can create a file.

Example: *cat >testy*

```
jan@jan-virtual-machine:~/Desktop$ cat > testy
This is a text file created from cat >
```

Note: To exit, press Ctrl + D

The cat command can be used with 2 familiar commands we used earlier. The **less** and **more** commands.

Example: *cat test.txt | more*

```
jan@jan-virtual-machine:~/Desktop$ cat test.txt | more
    1. This is a test 1
    2. This is a test 1
    3. This is a test 1
    4. This is a test 1
    5. This is a test 1
    6. This is a test 1
    7. This is a test 1
    8. This is a test 1
    9. This is a test 1
    10. This is a test 1
    11. This is a test 1
--More--
```

Example: *cat test.txt | less*

```
File  Edit  View  Search  Terminal  Help
<U+FEFF>        1. This is a test 1
      2. This is a test 1
      3. This is a test 1
      4. This is a test 1
      5. This is a test 1
      6. This is a test 1
      7. This is a test 1
      8. This is a test 1
      9. This is a test 1
      10. This is a test 1
      11. This is a test 1
      12. This is a test 1
:
```

Example: Displaying a line number with cat.
Command: *cat -n testx.txt*

```
jan@jan-virtual-machine:~/Desktop$ cat -n testx.txt
     1  This is a test 1
     2  This is a test 1
     3  This is a test 1
     4  This is a test 1
     5  This is a test 1
     6  This is a test 1
     7  This is a test 1
```

Overwriting the Files with cat - You can use the **redirection (standard input) operator (>)**. The following command will overwrite the text file. This is a useful tool, but you have to use it with caution. This can be performed for multiple files to obtain a single file.

Example: *cat test.txt > testx.txt*

Appending file content with cat without overwriting – Since the previous command causes overwriting, it cannot be used if you are willing to append a content from one file to another.

Example: cat *textx.txt >> testy.txt*

```
jan@jan-virtual-machine:~/Desktop$ cat testx.txt
     1. This is a test 1
     2. This is a test 1
jan@jan-virtual-machine:~/Desktop$ cat testy
This is a text file created from cat >jan@jan-virtual-machine:~/Desktop$
jan@jan-virtual-machine:~/Desktop$ cat testx.txt >> testy
jan@jan-virtual-machine:~/Desktop$ cat testy
This is a text file created from cat >     1. This is a test 1
     2. This is a test 1
jan@jan-virtual-machine:~/Desktop$
```

Example: Using standard input with cat.
Command: cat < testy

```
jan@jan-virtual-machine:~/Desktop$ cat < testy
This is a text file created from cat >     1. This is a test 1
     2. This is a test 1
jan@jan-virtual-machine:~/Desktop$
```

Using head and tail commands

By default, the head command displays 10 lines from the top and tail command displays the 10 lines from the bottom.

Examples:

- *head testy*
- *tail testy*
- *head -2 testy*
- *tail -2 testy*

```
jan@jan-virtual-machine:~/Desktop$ head test.txt
    1. This is a test 1
    2. This is a test 1
    3. This is a test 1
    4. This is a test 1
    5. This is a test 1
    6. This is a test 1
    7. This is a test 1
    8. This is a test 1
    9. This is a test 1
    10. This is a test 1
```

```
jan@jan-virtual-machine:~/Desktop$ tail test.txt
    40. This is a test 1
    41. This is a test 1
    42. This is a test 1
    43. This is a test 1
    44. This is a test 1
    45. This is a test 1
    46. This is a test 1
    47. This is a test 1
    48. This is a test 1
    49. This is a test 1
jan@jan-virtual-machine:~/Desktop$ head -2 test.txt
    1. This is a test 1
    2. This is a test 1
jan@jan-virtual-machine:~/Desktop$ tail -2 test.txt
    48. This is a test 1
    49. This is a test 1
jan@jan-virtual-machine:~/Desktop$ 
```

CHAPTER 6: Working with Disk, Media and Data Files

In this chapter you will learn

> Working with Disks and Partitions
>
> Working with data files
>
> Sorting
>
> Searching with grep
>
> Compressing files

In this chapter, we will be looking into some advanced commands to monitor basic disk properties, manage media files, such as mounting and unmounting, and to learn how to manage data files with more advanced commands.

Working with Disks

In the previous chapter, we discussed how Linux treats the file system and what the defaults files are. We will briefly look into the Linux disk formats and file systems.

Linux distributions run on the following disk formats.

- ext2.
- ext3.
- ext4.
- jfs.
- ReiserFS.
- XFS.
- Btrfs.

ext2, 3, and 4

This is the most used Linux file system nowadays. ext is a successor of Extended Filesystem (etc). The second version added more improvements and addressed limitations of the ext version (used in MINIX systems). It extended the size to 16 GB to 2 TB. ext2 is often used with removable media. The biggest improvement was the journaling capability. Linux kernel 2.4.15 integrated the ext2 file system. The leap was a major relief as it was very stable and did not need to check the disk once the machine goes through a clean shutdown. The upgrade capability from ext2 to ext3 was flawless. The third version extended the capabilities and the fourth version focused on performance standards. ext4 is the current version. This was released with the kernel version 2.6.28 and offered backward compatibility. It supports 16 GB to 16 TB maximum size and provides a mechanism to turn off journaling.

JFS

The Journaling File System was developed by IBM for AIX UNIX. It can be used as an alternative to ex4 when there are minimal system resources, especially the processing power.

ReiserFS

RFS is introduced as an alternative to ext3 with more advanced features and performance. It also has a faster journaling system.

XFS

It is a high speed JFS with parallel I/O processing.

In the previous chapters, the logical volume manager (LVM) was introduced (the virtual file system). The following image is a view of the entire LVM file structure.

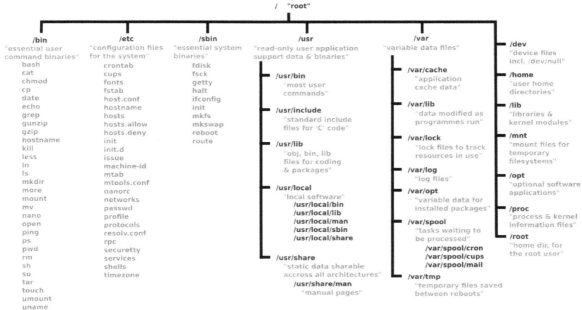

Image: Linux file system hierarchy

Source: https://en.wikipedia.org/wiki/Unix_filesystem

Working with Disks and Media

Mounting Media

Mounting is the technique of integrating the media to the virtual file system. It must be accomplished before accessing the media. Some systems support automatic mounting, but it is good to know how to mount the media manually.

The **mount** command is used to achieve this goal.

Syntax: *mount -t type device dir*

Other Syntaxes:

mount -a [-fFnrsvw] [-t vfstype] [-O optlist]

mount [-fnrsvw] [-o option[,option]...] device|dir

mount [-fnrsvw] [-t vfstype] [-o options] device|dir

The **umount** command can be used to unmount the command. Syntaxes are as follows.

umount [-hV]

umount -a [-dflnrv] [-t vfstype] [-O options]

umount [-dflnrv] {dir|device}...

Standard Command: *mount -t type device dir*

This command tells the *kernel* to attach the *filesystem/device* found in the *device* at the directory *dir*. When we issue a command, the mount command refers the /etc/fstab. This may contain information about what devices are often mounted, where, and using which options.

The mount command provides the following information.

-   The device file name.
-   The mount point in the virtual directory.
-   Filesystem type.
-   The access status.

The type depends on the many files systems available. In many cases, vfat is the file system mostly used (Windows long file system). Or else it can be a CD rom with the ISO9660.

Examples:

- *mount -t vfat /dev/vdb1 /mnt*
- *mount /cd or mount /dev/cdrom*

Automount Media

How do we automount something at start up? This is also a useful technique.

sudo mkdir /media/data #creates a directory in media to hold data.

sudo mount /dev/sdb1 /media/data #creates mount point and points to data.

ls -al /dev/disk/by-uuid/ #this command finds the UUID of the drive. Copy it.

sudo nano /etc/fstab #open fstab to add the UUID and mountpoint.

Add the following line at the end of the file, save and exit:

UUID=<The UUDI you copied> /media/data   ext4   defaults   0   0

Test if automount works: *sudo mount -a*

If nothing returns, you are good to go.

Dismounting Media

The last part is the dismounting process. There is a simple command to dismount. Can you guess?

umount

Syntax:

mount [-hV]

umount -a [-dflnrv] [-t vfstype] [-O options]

umount [-dflnrv] {dir|device}...

Examples:

- *umount /mnt*
- Force is the device is busy (be cautious about data losses): *umount -f /mnt*
- If it takes time, use the **lazy** option: *umount -l /mnt*

There is a great article to learn more about the mount/umount commands, hosted at https://www.computerhope.com/unix/umount.htm

Disk Space

In day to day tasks, you often need to find out the remaining disk space available in the individual device. The command to use in this occasion is **df**. du stands for Disk Free.

Syntax: *df [OPTION]... [FILE]...*

Options:

-a, −all : includes pseudo, duplicate and inaccessible file systems.

-B, −block-size=SIZE : scales sizes by SIZE before printing them.

-h, −human-readable : print sizes in power of 1024

-H, −si: print sizes in power of 1000

-i, −inodes : list inode information instead of block usage

-l, −local : limit listing to local file systems

-P, −portability : use POSIX output format

−sync : invoke sync before getting usage info

−total : elide all entries insignificant to available space, and produce grand total

-t, −type=TYPE : limit listing to file systems of type TYPE

-T, −print-type : print file system type

Examples:

- Display the size of all the files: *df -a*

- Display the size of home directory of someone: df /home/username (replace the username with the user's user name).

```
jan@jan-virtual-machine:~/Desktop$ df /home/jan
Filesystem      1K-blocks      Used Available Use% Mounted on
/dev/sda1       20509264   5544404  13900004  29% /
```

- Display the size of a file. This time in a more human readable format in bytes, KB, MB and GB.

```
jan@jan-virtual-machine:~/Desktop$ df -h Test1
Filesystem      Size  Used Avail Use% Mounted on
/dev/sda1        20G  5.3G   14G  29% /
```

- Print the size in the power of 1000s.

```
jan@jan-virtual-machine:~/Desktop$ df -H Test1
Filesystem      Size  Used Avail Use% Mounted on
/dev/sda1        22G  5.7G   15G  29% /
```

- Display the grand total of the size in human readable format (1024 blocks).

```
jan@jan-virtual-machine:~/Desktop$ df -h --total
Filesystem      Size  Used Avail Use% Mounted on
udev            960M     0  960M   0% /dev
tmpfs           197M  1.8M  195M   1% /run
/dev/sda1        20G  5.3G   14G  29% /
tmpfs           984M     0  984M   0% /dev/shm
tmpfs           5.0M  4.0K  5.0M   1% /run/lock
tmpfs           984M     0  984M   0% /sys/fs/cgroup
/dev/loop0      1.0M  1.0M     0 100% /snap/gnome-logs/61
/dev/loop1      4.2M  4.2M     0 100% /snap/gnome-calculator/406
/dev/loop2       55M   55M     0 100% /snap/core18/1066
/dev/loop3       15M   15M     0 100% /snap/gnome-characters/296
/dev/loop4      150M  150M     0 100% /snap/gnome-3-28-1804/67
/dev/loop5       89M   89M     0 100% /snap/core/7270
/dev/loop7      3.8M  3.8M     0 100% /snap/gnome-system-monitor/100
/dev/loop6       43M   43M     0 100% /snap/gtk-common-themes/1313
tmpfs           197M   16K  197M   1% /run/user/121
tmpfs           197M   64K  197M   1% /run/user/1000
/dev/sr0         56M   56M     0 100% /media/jan/VMware Tools
vmhgfs-fuse     514G  435G   80G  85% /mnt/hgfs
tmpfs           197M     0  197M   0% /run/user/0
total           537G  440G   97G  83% -
```

- Display the file type: *df -T filename*

A similar command exists in order to find the disk usage. The command is **du**.

Syntax:

du [OPTION]... [FILE]...

du [OPTION]... --files0-from=F

Options: Some options are similar to the *df* command.

-0, —null : end each output line with NULL

-a, —all : write count of all files, not just directories

—apparent-size : print apparent sizes, rather than disk usage.

-B, —block-size=SIZE : scale sizes to SIZE before printing on console

-c, —total : produce grand total

-d, —max-depth=N : print total for directory only if it is N or fewer levels below command line argument

-h, —human-readable : print sizes in human readable format

-S, -separate-dirs : for directories, don't include size of subdirectories

-s, —summarize : display only total for each directory

—time : show time of of last modification of any file or directory.

—exclude=PATTERN : exclude files that match PATTERN

Examples:

- Disk usage summary of the home directory of a user: *du /home/jan*
- Viewing with human readable format.

```
jan@jan-virtual-machine:~/Desktop$ du -h
4.0K    ./Test
4.0K    ./Test2
28K     .
```

- Grand total of disk usage for any directory: *dh -sh*

```
jan@jan-virtual-machine:~/Desktop$ du -sh ./
28K     ./
```

- Disk usage for every file: du -a

- To get the disk usage of the files in a directory with the grand total: *du -ch*

```
jan@jan-virtual-machine:~/Desktop$ du -ch
4.0K      ./Test
4.0K      ./Test2
28K       .
28K       total
```

- Exclude certain files form the list. *du - ah --exclude*

```
jan@jan-virtual-machine:~/Desktop$ ls
sym  Test  Test1  Test2  test.txt  testx.txt  testy
jan@jan-virtual-machine:~/Desktop$ du -ah --exclude="*.txt"
4.0K      ./Test
4.0K      ./testy
4.0K      ./Test1
4.0K      ./Test2
0         ./sym
20K       .
```

- Disk usage based on the file modification time: *du -ah –time* /home/jan/Desktop

```
jan@jan-virtual-machine:~/Desktop$ du -ah --time ./
4.0K      2019-09-18 17:17      ./Test
4.0K      2019-09-18 18:03      ./testy
4.0K      2019-09-18 17:47      ./test.txt
4.0K      2019-09-18 18:02      ./testx.txt
4.0K      2019-09-18 17:15      ./Test1
4.0K      2019-09-20 00:19      ./Test2
0         2019-09-18 17:17      ./sym
28K       2019-09-20 00:19      ./
```

Obtaining Disk Partition Information

The command to use is lsblk. This stands for "list block devices". An example is below.

```
jan@jan-virtual-machine:~/Desktop$ lsblk
NAME     MAJ:MIN RM    SIZE RO TYPE MOUNTPOINT
loop0      7:0     0   1008K  1 loop /snap/gnome-logs/61
loop1      7:1     0      4M  1 loop /snap/gnome-calculator/406
loop2      7:2     0   54.4M  1 loop /snap/core18/1066
loop3      7:3     0   14.8M  1 loop /snap/gnome-characters/296
loop4      7:4     0  149.9M  1 loop /snap/gnome-3-28-1804/67
loop5      7:5     0   88.5M  1 loop /snap/core/7270
loop6      7:6     0   42.8M  1 loop /snap/gtk-common-themes/1313
loop7      7:7     0    3.7M  1 loop /snap/gnome-system-monitor/100
sda        8:0     0    20G   0 disk
└─sda1     8:1     0    20G   0 part /
sr0       11:0     1   55.9M  0 rom  /media/jan/VMware Tools
```

To view disk and partition information, use the following commands. Although these commands have more uses its out of scope of this book.

Disk Information

View Partition Description – Command: *sudo fdisk -l*

```
Disk /dev/sda: 20 GiB, 21474836480 bytes, 41943040 sectors
Units: sectors of 1 * 512 = 512 bytes
Sector size (logical/physical): 512 bytes / 512 bytes
I/O size (minimum/optimal): 512 bytes / 512 bytes
Disklabel type: dos
Disk identifier: 0x5d7e615b

Device     Boot Start      End  Sectors Size Id Type
/dev/sda1  *    2048 41940991 41938944  20G 83 Linux
```

View Partition Information – Command: sudo parted -l

```
Model: VMware, VMware Virtual S (scsi)
Disk /dev/sda: 21.5GB
Sector size (logical/physical): 512B/512B
Partition Table: msdos
Disk Flags:

Number  Start    End     Size    Type     File system  Flags
 1      1049kB   21.5GB  21.5GB  primary  ext4         boot
```

Working with Data Files

In this section, we will look into the commands which are used to manipulate and organize data.

Sorting Data

Sorting is one of the most convenient uses of data when it comes to human understandable formats. Sorting can be done according to many patterns. For instance, from A-Z, or a-z, ascending or descending. Let's look at an example. The command is as you guessed, **sort**.

```
jan@jan-virtual-machine:~/Desktop$ sort File1
1
10
2
3
4
5
6
7
8
9
jan@jan-virtual-machine:~/Desktop$ sort File2
Apr
Aug
Dec
Feb
Jan
July
June
Mar
Nov
Oct
Sept
```

What happened here? As you see, it relies on basic rules, such as language rules. In the first example, 1 and 0 together 1+0 is sorted like 1, then 10 then 100 and so on. If we take a look at this example, it will be easier to understand.

```
jan@jan-virtual-machine:~/Desktop$ sort File1

1
10
100
12
120
2
3
4
5
6
7
8
9
```

As you see, it requires more clear instructions to distinguish between the general rules and more specific rules.

Syntax: *sort [OPTION]... [FILE]...*

sort [OPTION]... --file0-from=F

Options: Sorting command comes with a lot of options. See *man sort* for more. These options are self-explanatory. Let's look at some examples.

Example: Sorting by numerical values.

Command: *sort -n File1*

```
jan@jan-virtual-machine:~/Desktop$ sort -n File1

1
2
3
4
5
6
7
8
9
10
12
100
120
```

Example: Sort by Months

Command: *sort -M File2*

```
jan@jan-virtual-machine:~/Desktop$ sort -M File2
APR
AUG
DEC
FEB
JAN
JUL
JUN
MAR
MAY
NOV
OCT
SEP
```

You would say, "Wow! It does not work!"

What is causing the file not to be sorted according to English? **If your system uses a different language than English, then this command will not work!**

In order to fix this, you have to change the format of the selected Language by accessing the settings panel.

Image: Changing the default format

If the format is a non-English speaking country, change it to an appropriate format (in my case, I have selected United States). This must be followed by a restart.

Voila! It worked!

Another example is using the reverse order with the **-r** option.

When we sort, we can specify a position to start with. This is useful when a data file has many positions. For instance, let's look at the /etc/passwd/

It has many lines similar to this. Let's assume you want to sort by the 3rd field. Here we will select a field separator and it is ':'. To specify the field position, use the -k parameter. To specify the field separator, use the -t parameter accordingly. The sorting format is numeric. The example attempts to sort the passwd file by numeric user id.

Before:

```
root:x:0:0:root:/root:/bin/bash
daemon:x:1:1:daemon:/usr/sbin:/usr/sbin/nologin
bin:x:2:2:bin:/bin:/usr/sbin/nologin
sys:x:3:3:sys:/dev:/usr/sbin/nologin
sync:x:4:65534:sync:/bin:/bin/sync
games:x:5:60:games:/usr/games:/usr/sbin/nologin
man:x:6:12:man:/var/cache/man:/usr/sbin/nologin
lp:x:7:7:lp:/var/spool/lpd:/usr/sbin/nologin
mail:x:8:8:mail:/var/mail:/usr/sbin/nologin
news:x:9:9:news:/var/spool/news:/usr/sbin/nologin
uucp:x:10:10:uucp:/var/spool/uucp:/usr/sbin/nologin
proxy:x:13:13:proxy:/bin:/usr/sbin/nologin
www-data:x:33:33:www-data:/var/www:/usr/sbin/nologin
backup:x:34:34:backup:/var/backups:/usr/sbin/nologin
list:x:38:38:Mailing List Manager:/var/list:/usr/sbin/nologin
irc:x:39:39:ircd:/var/run/ircd:/usr/sbin/nologin
gnats:x:41:41:Gnats Bug-Reporting System (admin):/var/lib/gnats:/usr/sbin/nologi
n
nobody:x:65534:65534:nobody:/nonexistent:/usr/sbin/nologin
systemd-network:x:100:102:systemd Network Management,,,:/run/systemd/netif:/usr/
sbin/nologin
```

After *sort -t ':' -k 3 -n /etc/passwd*:

```
jan@jan-virtual-machine:~/Desktop$ sort -t ':' -k 3 -n /etc/passwd
root:x:0:0:root:/root:/bin/bash
daemon:x:1:1:daemon:/usr/sbin:/usr/sbin/nologin
bin:x:2:2:bin:/bin:/usr/sbin/nologin
sys:x:3:3:sys:/dev:/usr/sbin/nologin
sync:x:4:65534:sync:/bin:/bin/sync
games:x:5:60:games:/usr/games:/usr/sbin/nologin
man:x:6:12:man:/var/cache/man:/usr/sbin/nologin
lp:x:7:7:lp:/var/spool/lpd:/usr/sbin/nologin
mail:x:8:8:mail:/var/mail:/usr/sbin/nologin
news:x:9:9:news:/var/spool/news:/usr/sbin/nologin
uucp:x:10:10:uucp:/var/spool/uucp:/usr/sbin/nologin
proxy:x:13:13:proxy:/bin:/usr/sbin/nologin
www-data:x:33:33:www-data:/var/www:/usr/sbin/nologin
backup:x:34:34:backup:/var/backups:/usr/sbin/nologin
list:x:38:38:Mailing List Manager:/var/list:/usr/sbin/nologin
irc:x:39:39:ircd:/var/run/ircd:/usr/sbin/nologin
gnats:x:41:41:Gnats Bug-Reporting System (admin):/var/lib/gnats:/usr/sbin/nologi
n
systemd-network:x:100:102:systemd Network Management,,,:/run/systemd/netif:/usr/
sbin/nologin
systemd-resolve:x:101:103:systemd Resolver,,,:/run/systemd/resolve:/usr/sbin/nol
ogin
```

It is well sorted now.

Let's use some previous commands in conjunction with sort command.

Sort by Disk Space example: *du -sh /home/jan | sort -nr*

Here, **r** indicates reverse sort. This command (du) used to obtain a grand total of disk usage, sort numerically in reverse order, and then displays the top 10 lines (by default head command returns the top 10 lines).

```
jan@jan-virtual-machine:/bin$ du -sh * | sort -nr | head
732K    brltty
572K    udevadm
544K    ip
416K    tar
244K    nano
216K    grep
208K    loadkeys
196K    hciconfig
180K    systemctl
168K    less
```

Using Disk Free and Sort Command

In this example, df -h | sort -r -k 5 -I is able to sort the disk usage by the percentage of use.

Before: *df -h*

```
jan@jan-virtual-machine:/bin$ df -h
Filesystem      Size  Used Avail Use% Mounted on
udev            960M     0  960M   0% /dev
tmpfs           197M  1.8M  195M   1% /run
/dev/sda1        20G  5.3G   14G  29% /
tmpfs           984M     0  984M   0% /dev/shm
tmpfs           5.0M  4.0K  5.0M   1% /run/lock
tmpfs           984M     0  984M   0% /sys/fs/cgroup
/dev/loop1       55M   55M     0 100% /snap/core18/1066
/dev/loop0       15M   15M     0 100% /snap/gnome-characters/296
/dev/loop3      3.8M  3.8M     0 100% /snap/gnome-system-monitor/100
/dev/loop6       43M   43M     0 100% /snap/gtk-common-themes/1313
/dev/loop4      1.0M  1.0M     0 100% /snap/gnome-logs/61
/dev/loop5       89M   89M     0 100% /snap/core/7270
/dev/loop2      150M  150M     0 100% /snap/gnome-3-28-1804/67
/dev/loop7      4.2M  4.2M     0 100% /snap/gnome-calculator/406
tmpfs           197M   20K  197M   1% /run/user/121
vmhgfs-fuse     514G  430G   84G  84% /mnt/hgfs
tmpfs           197M   44K  197M   1% /run/user/1000
```

After: *df -h | sort -nrk 5*

```
jan@jan-virtual-machine:~/Desktop$ df -h | sort -nrk 5
/dev/loop7      4.2M  4.2M      0 100% /snap/gnome-calculator/406
/dev/loop6       43M   43M      0 100% /snap/gtk-common-themes/1313
/dev/loop5       89M   89M      0 100% /snap/core/7270
/dev/loop4      1.0M  1.0M      0 100% /snap/gnome-logs/61
/dev/loop3      3.8M  3.8M      0 100% /snap/gnome-system-monitor/100
/dev/loop2      150M  150M      0 100% /snap/gnome-3-28-1804/67
/dev/loop1       55M   55M      0 100% /snap/core18/1066
/dev/loop0       15M   15M      0 100% /snap/gnome-characters/296
vmhgfs-fuse     514G  430G    84G  84% /mnt/hgfs
/dev/sda1        20G  5.3G    14G  29% /
tmpfs           5.0M  4.0K   5.0M   1% /run/lock
tmpfs           197M   44K   197M   1% /run/user/1000
tmpfs           197M   20K   197M   1% /run/user/121
tmpfs           197M  1.8M   195M   1% /run
udev            960M     0   960M   0% /dev
tmpfs           984M     0   984M   0% /sys/fs/cgroup
tmpfs           984M     0   984M   0% /dev/shm
Filesystem      Size  Used  Avail Use% Mounted on
```

As you see here, according to 5th field, it is sorted.

Sorting command provides 3 advanced features.

- Evaluating if a file is unsorted. For this use the -c option. We use sort -cn command to find out if the file is sorted. It detects the first disorder at the 6th line as 12 is out of order. This is also true for other sorting options including months.

```
jan@jan-virtual-machine:~/Desktop$ cat File1
1
2
4
10
100
12
120
5
8
3
6
9
7
jan@jan-virtual-machine:~/Desktop$ sort -cn File1
sort: File1:6: disorder: 12
```

- We can remove duplicates when we use the option **-u**. Let's use the command *sort -un File1*

```
jan@jan-virtual-machine:~/Desktop$ cat File1
1
2
4
10
12
120
2
10
5
4
jan@jan-virtual-machine:~/Desktop$ sort -un File1

1
2
4
5
10
12
120
```

- Finally, the sort command can be used to send the output to a new file. This is also a great option. Let's use the previous command. The new command would be sort -un File1 > File3.txt

```
jan@jan-virtual-machine:~/Desktop$ sort -un File1 > File3.txt
jan@jan-virtual-machine:~/Desktop$ cat File3.txt

1
2
4
5
10
12
120
```

When it comes to data handling, the most important is undoubtedly the **searching capability**. Now we are going to look at the grep command.

Searching with grep

Searching within data is one of the most important tasks of any person who is using a computer and engaging with data handling. To find a specific word or a line of text within a file without scrolling for hours can really save the time of yours and the organization's you work for. It has many useful options as well. Do not confuse searching for data with searching for files.

Grep is capable of using many options and search patterns. It can even use colors for the output (match).

Syntax: *grep [OPTIONS] PATTERN [FILE...]*

Options: For options, execute the *man grep* command.

In the first example, we will simply look for a word "That" in an html file.

Command: grep --color "that" filename.html

As you see, the output is colored with this command,

```
jan@jan-virtual-machine:~/Desktop$ grep --color "That" Wikipedia_Wikipedia\ reco
rds\ -\ Wikipedia.html
<li>First <a href="https://en.wikipedia.org/wiki/Special:PermanentLink/11992008"
 title="Special:PermanentLink/11992008">named user</a>: <a href="https://en.wiki
pedia.org/wiki/User:ScottMoonen" title="User:ScottMoonen">ScottMoonen</a> on 16
January 2001.<sup id="cite_ref-1" class="reference"><a href="https://en.wikipedi
a.org/wiki/Wikipedia:Wikipedia_records#cite_note-1">[1]</a></sup> That diff, wit
h "about me", also has the record for Wikipedia's first ever <a href="https://en
.wikipedia.org/wiki/Help:Edit_summary" title="Help:Edit summary">edit summary</a
>.
<ul><li>That is a list or timeline: <a href="https://en.wikipedia.org/wiki/Timel
ine_of_Russian_interference_in_the_2016_United_States_elections" title="Timeline
 of Russian interference in the 2016 United States elections">Timeline of Russia
n interference in the 2016 United States elections</a> (484,764 bytes as of 14 A
ugust 2019)</li>
<li>That is not a list or timeline: <a href="https://en.wikipedia.org/wiki/Saudi
_Arabian-led_intervention_in_Yemen" title="Saudi Arabian-led intervention in Yem
en">Saudi Arabian-led intervention in Yemen</a> (439,866 as of 14 August 2019)</
li>
<li>That is a biography: <a href="https://en.wikipedia.org/wiki/Donald_Trump" ti
```

To view line numbers, use the **-n** option.

Command: *grep -n --color "Wikipedia" Wikipedia_Wikipedia\ records\ -\ Wikipedia.html*

```
jan@jan-virtual-machine:~/Desktop$ grep -n --color "Wikipedia" Wikipedia_Wikipedia\ records\ -\ Wikipedia.html
2:<!-- saved from url=(0057)https://en.wikipedia.org/wiki/Wikipedia:Wikipedia_records -->
5:<title>Wikipedia:Wikipedia records - Wikipedia</title>
6:<script>document.documentElement.className=document.documentElement.className.replace(/(^|\s)client-nojs(\s|$
spaceNumber":4,"wgPageName":"Wikipedia:Wikipedia_records","wgTitle":"Wikipedia records","wgCurRevisionId":91572
iew","wgUserName":null,"wgUserGroups":["*"],"wgCategories":["Wikipedia statistics","Wikipedia history"],"wgBrea
:["",""],"wgDigitTransformTable":["",""],"wgDefaultDateFormat":"dmy","wgMonthNames":["","January","February","M
sShort":["","Jan","Feb","Mar","Apr","May","Jun","Jul","Aug","Sep","Oct","Nov","Dec"],"wgRelevantPageName":"Wiki
12:<link rel="stylesheet" href="./Wikipedia_Wikipedia records - Wikipedia_files/load.php">
13:<link rel="stylesheet" href="./Wikipedia_Wikipedia records - Wikipedia_files/load(1).php">
14:<script async="" src="./Wikipedia_Wikipedia records - Wikipedia_files/load(2).php"></script>
39:<link rel="stylesheet" href="./Wikipedia_Wikipedia records - Wikipedia_files/load(3).php">
```

To perform case insensitive search, use **-i** option.

Command: *grep -ni --color "Wikipedia" Wikipedia_Wikipedia\ records\ -\ Wikipedia.html*

```
83:<ul><li><a href="https://en.wikipedia.org/wiki/Wikipedia:Statistics" title="W
ikipedia:Statistics">General info</a></li>
84:<li><a href="https://en.wikipedia.org/wiki/Special:Statistics" title="Special
```

If there are multiple files, you can search all the files with the use of wildcards such as '*'.

Command: *grep -in --color "Apr" *.txt*

```
jan@jan-virtual-machine:~/Desktop$ grep -ni --color "Apr" *.txt
File2.txt:1:APR
File2.txt:13:APR
File2.txt:15:APR
File3.txt:4:APR
File3.txt:6:APR
```

You can also search subdirectories recursively with **-r**.

Command: *grep -in --color "Apr" ***

```
jan@jan-virtual-machine:~/Desktop$ grep -inr --color "Apr" *
File2.txt:1:APR
File2.txt:13:APR
File2.txt:15:APR
File3.txt:4:APR
File3.txt:6:APR
Test/File5.txt:1:APR
Test/File5.txt:13:APR
Test/File5.txt:15:APR
Test2/File6.txt:1:APR
Test2/File6.txt:13:APR
Test2/File6.txt:15:APR
```

Using Regular Expressions

Example: Here we are using the wildcard '.' To represent any character that will be matched. '*' means any character or number of characters. In this case, if we take a match "Your.*account", the qualified words are any word or sentence in between the 'Your' and 'account'. It can be "Your bank account" or "Youraccount". Since we use -in this won't be looking for cases.

Command: *grep -inr --color "Your.*account" *.txt*

```
jan@jan-virtual-machine:~/Desktop$ grep -i -n -r --color "Your.*account" *.txt
File1.txt:1:Your bank account.
File1.txt:3:Your trusted account.
File1.txt:4:This is your account.
File1.txt:5:This is far into your own account.
File2.txt:1:I am not going to put this into your account. However, you must be r
esponsible for the sake of the protection of your bank account.
```

There are lots of uses with grep command and we will be using it more in the next few chapters.

Using Gzip, Bzip2 and Tar

The gzip and bzip2 are commonly used for file compression and decompression. If you are a Windows user, you must be familiar with WinZip and WinRAR or even 7Zip. These command-line utilities do the same. However, the gzip command uses Lempel-Ziv algorithm and is found in some Microsoft algorithms. The other users Burrows-Wheeler block sorting algorithm. Let's take an example for each algorithm.

```
jan@jan-virtual-machine:~/Desktop$ ls -lh File1.txt
-rw-rw-r-- 1 jan jan 168K Sep 22 23:56 File1.txt
jan@jan-virtual-machine:~/Desktop$ gzip File1.txt
jan@jan-virtual-machine:~/Desktop$ ls -lh File1.txt.gz
-rw-rw-r-- 1 jan jan 749 Sep 22 23:56 File1.txt.gz
```

Here you can see the original file size has reduced to a significant low size (168K to 749 Bytes).

```
jan@jan-virtual-machine:~/Desktop$ ls -lh File11.txt
-rw-rw-r-- 1 jan jan 168K Sep 22 23:56 File11.txt
jan@jan-virtual-machine:~/Desktop$ bzip2 File11.txt
jan@jan-virtual-machine:~/Desktop$ ls -lh File
File11.txt.bz2  File1.txt.gz   File2.txt      File3.txt
jan@jan-virtual-machine:~/Desktop$ ls -lh File11.txt.bz2
-rw-rw-r-- 1 jan jan 242 Sep 22 23:56 File11.txt.bz2
```

With bzip2 the compression is even higher than gzip.

Also note, the compressed file can be compressed with another algorithm. For instance, we could compress the gzip file again with bzip2.

```
jan@jan-virtual-machine:~/Desktop$ ls -lh File1.txt.gz
-rw-rw-r-- 1 jan jan 749 Sep 22 23:56 File1.txt.gz
jan@jan-virtual-machine:~/Desktop$ bzip2 File1.txt.gz
jan@jan-virtual-machine:~/Desktop$ ls -lh File1.txt.gz.bz2
-rw-rw-r-- 1 jan jan 327 Sep 22 23:56 File1.txt.gz.bz2
```

Here, the drawback is clearly visible. The direct bzip2 application was far more efficient.

To decompress, use the -d option.

```
jan@jan-virtual-machine:~/Desktop$ bzip2 -d File1.txt.gz.bz2
jan@jan-virtual-machine:~/Desktop$ gzip -d File1.txt.gz
```

There is a significant issue with these utilities. Those replace the original file (deletes). To prevent it, use the -k option (keep).

bzip2 -k File1.txt

```
jan@jan-virtual-machine:~/Desktop$ bzip2 -k File1.txt
jan@jan-virtual-machine:~/Desktop$ ls -lh File1
File11.txt.bz2   File1.txt        File1.txt.bz2
```

As you are able to see, the original file is still there.

tar

The tar command was developed with the original intention of archiving files. Nowadays, it is used for data collection and backing up data.

Tar is used in conjunction with gzip and bzip2. The resulting file are tar.gz or something similar. These are called **tar balls**. The purpose of tar is to archive and compress the output files. This is also useful for backing up files.

tar [-] A --catenate --concatenate | c --create | d --diff --compare |

  --delete | r --append | t --list | --test-label | u --update |

  x --extract --get [options] [pathname ...]

Example: *tar -czvf archive_name.tar.gz /path/to/file-or-directory*

Command: *tar -czvf archive.tar.gz Test*

```
jan@jan-virtual-machine:~/Desktop$ bzip2 File1.txt File1.bz2
bzip2: Can't open input file File1.bz2: No such file or directory.
jan@jan-virtual-machine:~/Desktop$ tar -czvf archive.tar.gz Test
Test/
Test/File5.txt
```

You can also list multiple files or directories: /home/jan/Desktop/Test /home/jan/Desktop/Test1 etc.

Another feature is excluding files or directories: *tar -czvf archive.tar.gz ./ -- exclude=File11.txt.bz2 --exclude=File1.txt.bz2*

```
jan@jan-virtual-machine:~/Desktop$ tar -czvf archive.tar.gz ./ --exclude=File11.
txt.bz2 --exclude=File1.txt.bz2
./
./File2.txt
./Test/
./Test/File5.txt
./File1.txt.bz2
./File3.txt
./File11.txt.bz2
./Test2/
./Test2/File6.txt
```

Here I am excluding 2 archives from the tar.

To untar, use the following command.

Command: *tar -xzvf archive.tar.gz*

CHAPTER 7: Shell Scripting: Visiting Prerequisites

In this chapter you will learn

      Process management

      Bash commands

      Environment Variables

Before we get into the scripting deeper, we have to learn few more certain advanced features.

-    Processes and Relationships.
-    Environment Variables.

Process Management Basics

Let's explore the shell. As you learned in the previous chapters, there are several shell types. To find the shell type you can use this example.

Command: *cat /etc/passwd*

```
jan:x:1000:1000:Jan,,,:/home/jan:/bin/bash
```

This executable resides on /bin. There are other shells as well. You can find this information using *ls -lF /bin/bash*. You can find other shells using /csh, /dash etc. The following example demonstrates this task.

```
jan@jan-virtual-machine:~/Desktop$ ls -lF /bin/bash
-rwxr-xr-x 1 root root 1113504 Jun  7 03:58 /bin/bash*
```

Parent Child Relationship

As stated in a previous section, the bash shell starts either when you log into the text-mode interface or when you launch a terminal in GUI. This is what we called a **parent shell**. If we run a bash command or something related, it spawns another shell, which is a child of the parent shell and it also has a prompt and acts like the parent.

To examine this process, we are using a special command. It is the **ps** (process status) command.

```
jan@jan-virtual-machine:~/Desktop$ ps -f
UID          PID    PPID  C STIME TTY          TIME CMD
jan         4142    4133  0 22:23 pts/0     00:00:00 bash
jan         4245    4142  0 23:17 pts/0     00:00:00 ps -f
```

```
jan@jan-virtual-machine:~/Desktop$ bash
jan@jan-virtual-machine:~/Desktop$ ps -f
UID          PID    PPID  C STIME TTY          TIME CMD
jan         4142    4133  0 22:23 pts/0     00:00:00 bash
jan         4249    4142  0 23:20 pts/0     00:00:00 bash
jan         4257    4249  0 23:20 pts/0     00:00:00 ps -f
```

Here the UID stands for User ID, PID is Process ID, PPID is Parent Process ID, C is Process Utilization, STIME is Start Time, TTY is Time to Live, Time is Total Time and finally the command executed.

Here in the first image you see the first command *ps -f*. Before that the bash is running and its process ID was 4142. The other was the actual *ps -f* command.

Once we execute the bash command, it displays a set of new processes. The 2nd line of the 2nd image shows a child process under the parent bash shell. The process ID of the parent bash was 4142. The child bash process has 4249 as the PID. The next *ps* command executes in this shell. To see this in the terminal in a graphical representation we can use the **--forest** option with the **ps** command.

```
jan@jan-virtual-machine:~/Desktop$ ps --forest
  PID TTY          TIME CMD
 4142 pts/0     00:00:00 bash
 4249 pts/0     00:00:00  \_ bash
 4272 pts/0     00:00:00      \_ ps
```

We call this parent child process **Sub-shelling**. The ps command is a powerful process information utility and it can be used to examine the nesting and shell processing.

Bash Command Parameters

Table: Bash command parameters

Parameters	Description
-c \<string>	Reads commands (from a string)
-i	Interactive shell. This accepts user inputs.
-l	Act as if invoked as login shell
-r	Restrict the shell to the users to the default directory
-s	Reads commands from the user's input

To exit from the shells (child and parent), issue the **exit** command.

To understand this in more detail, let's look at this example. Let's issue a list of commands to execute one by one.

ls; pwd; cd ..; pwd; ls;

Now, let's verify if the command spawned a subshell. Although we are going to learn more about environment variables in the next lesson, we will use an environment variable. It is $BASH_SUBSHELL.

Let's use it with the first example.

ls; pwd; cd ..; pwd; ls; echo $BASH_SUBSHELL

```
jan@jan-virtual-machine:/home$ ls; pwd; cd ..; pwd; ls; echo $BASH_SUBSHELL
jake  jan  test2
/home
/
bin    dev   initrd.img      lib64        mnt   root  snap       sys   var
boot   etc   initrd.img.old  lost+found   opt   run   srv        tmp   vmlinuz
cdrom  home  lib             media        proc  sbin  swapfile   usr
0
```

Focus on the last line where there is a 0.

Now, let's run the same command with a slight modification.

(ls; pwd; cd ..; pwd; ls;)

```
jan@jan-virtual-machine:/$ (ls; pwd; cd ..; pwd; ls;)
bin     dev     initrd.img       lib64        mnt     root    snap       sys   var
boot    etc     initrd.img.old   lost+found   opt     run     srv        tmp   vmlinuz
cdrom   home    lib              media        proc    sbin    swapfile   usr
/
/
bin     dev     initrd.img       lib64        mnt     root    snap       sys   var
boot    etc     initrd.img.old   lost+found   opt     run     srv        tmp   vmlinuz
cdrom   home    lib              media        proc    sbin    swapfile   usr
```

This seems normal except for the use of the brackets. However, there is a huge difference. The parentheses make the command run in a subshell. To identify this, let's run the following command.

(ls; pwd; cd ..; pwd; ls; echo $BASH_SUBSHELL)

```
jan@jan-virtual-machine:/$ (ls; pwd; cd ..; pwd; ls; echo $BASH_SUBSHELL)
bin     dev     initrd.img       lib64        mnt     root    snap       sys   var
boot    etc     initrd.img.old   lost+found   opt     run     srv        tmp   vmlinuz
cdrom   home    lib              media        proc    sbin    swapfile   usr
/
/
bin     dev     initrd.img       lib64        mnt     root    snap       sys   var
boot    etc     initrd.img.old   lost+found   opt     run     srv        tmp   vmlinuz
cdrom   home    lib              media        proc    sbin    swapfile   usr
1
```

Notice the change from 0 to 1 at the bottom.

If you use nested parentheses, what will be the result?

```
jan@jan-virtual-machine:/$ (pwd; ls; cd ..; (pwd; echo $BASH_SUBSHELL))
/
bin     dev     initrd.img       lib64        mnt     root    snap       sys   var
boot    etc     initrd.img.old   lost+found   opt     run     srv        tmp   vmlinuz
cdrom   home    lib              media        proc    sbin    swapfile   usr
/
2
```

Now you can see the formation of 2 subshells.

Subshells can be used effectively. Pipes, process lists, and co-processes subshells. You can use subshells effectively with the **background mode**. For instance, you can put a process in the background by using the **sleep** command. Let's look at an example.

sleep 10

This will sleep a process for 10 seconds in the foreground mode as you see your cursor has frozen and blinked for 10 seconds. To put a process in the background, use & with the same command.

sleep 1000&

Tip: A background job must return a process ID in order to identify it.

Let's use the *ps -f* to identify it.

```
jan@jan-virtual-machine:/$ sleep 1000&
[1] 4837
jan@jan-virtual-machine:/$ ps -f
UID          PID    PPID  C STIME TTY          TIME CMD
jan          4342   4333  0 07:59 pts/0    00:00:00 bash
jan          4837   4342  0 09:39 pts/0    00:00:00 sleep 1000
jan          4838   4342  0 09:39 pts/0    00:00:00 ps -f
```

The command returned the Job ID as well as Process ID. Now let's observe this **"job"** that is running in the background using the **jobs** command. When the job is running and when it is finished, we could see the following outputs.

jobs

```
jan@jan-virtual-machine:/$ jobs
[1]+  Running                 sleep 1000 &
```

```
jan@jan-virtual-machine:/$ jobs
[1]+  Done                    sleep 1000
```

To obtain some more information, use the *job -l* command.

Similarly, a set of processes can be put in the background mode. Let's take another example.

(sleep 10; echo $BASH_SUBSHELL; sleep 10) &

```
jan@jan-virtual-machine:/$ (sleep 10 ; echo $BASH_SUBSHELL ; sleep 10)&
[2] 4881
[1]   Done                    ( sleep 1-; echo $BASH_SUBSHELL; sleep 10 )
jan@jan-virtual-machine:/$
jan@jan-virtual-machine:/$ jobs
[2]+  Running                 ( sleep 10; echo $BASH_SUBSHELL; sleep 10 ) &
jan@jan-virtual-machine:/$ 1
```

Once the first is processed, you have to press the enter key once more.

```
jan@jan-virtual-machine:/$ 1

[2]+  Done                    ( sleep 10; echo $BASH_SUBSHELL; sleep 10 )
```

Now, it the status of the second process comes visible.

Using Co-processes

Co-processing is the technique to spawn a subshell and execute a command at once. The command to use here is **coproc**.

Example: Put a process to sleep and observe the behavior.

Command: *coproc sleep 10*

```
jan@jan-virtual-machine:/$ jobs
[1]+  Running                 coproc COPROC sleep 10 &
jan@jan-virtual-machine:/$ jobs
[1]+  Done                    coproc COPROC sleep 10
```

Internal and External Commands

In the Linux atmosphere, there are two types of commands: Internal and External.

External Commands

These are not built-in shell commands. These commands (a.k.a. file system commands), exist outside of the shell. These actually are programs or utilities. Therefore, these programs can be located in directories such as /bin, /sbin, usr/bin or usr/sbin.

The main different of external command is it requires to form or what we call **fork** in Linux terms, a child process to execute.

Internal Commands

These are the built-in shell commands. Internal commands do not require forking child processes.

To identify the type of the commands and where these reside, we can use the following commands. For instance,

- *which ps*
- *type -a ps*

```
jan@jan-virtual-machine:/$ which ps
/bin/ps
jan@jan-virtual-machine:/$ type -a ps
ps is /bin/ps
```

Let's find more information about this */bin/ps* by issuing, *ls -l /bin/ps*.

```
jan@jan-virtual-machine:/$ ls -l /bin/ps
-rwxr-xr-x 1 root root 133432 May 14  2018 /bin/ps
```

Now according to the information *ps* is an external command. What are the internal commands?

The commands, such as **echo,** are internal commands. Echo command simply echoes something back. To see a list of options, see *man echo*.

```
jan@jan-virtual-machine:/$ echo "Test"
Test
jan@jan-virtual-machine:/$ ps -f
UID        PID   PPID  C STIME TTY          TIME CMD
jan        4342  4333  0 07:59 pts/0    00:00:00 bash
jan        5155  4342  0 15:20 pts/0    00:00:00 ps -f
```

As you see echo does not return any child processes.

A comprehensive list of internal commands is available at
http://manpages.ubuntu.com/manpages/xenial/man7/bash-builtins.7.html

There are few other commands when controlling the processes. In this book, we are not going to look at *ps* commands in a system administrator's perspective. Let's look at the others instead.

- **bg**: Sends a process to the background (a stopped process is resumed).

```
jan@jan-virtual-machine:/$ sleep 100
^Z
[1]+  Stopped                 sleep 100
jan@jan-virtual-machine:/$ bg %1
[1]+ sleep 100 &
jan@jan-virtual-machine:/$ jobs -l
[1]+   5188 Running                 sleep 100 &
```

- **fg**: Resumes a process from background to foreground.

```
jan@jan-virtual-machine:/$ sleep 60 &
[1] 5172
jan@jan-virtual-machine:/$ ps -f
UID         PID   PPID  C STIME TTY          TIME CMD
jan        4342   4333  0 07:59 pts/0    00:00:00 bash
jan        5172   4342  0 15:34 pts/0    00:00:00 sleep 60
jan        5175   4342  0 15:34 pts/0    00:00:00 ps -f
jan@jan-virtual-machine:/$ fg %1
sleep 60
^Z
[1]+  Stopped                 sleep 60
jan@jan-virtual-machine:/$ jobs
[1]+  Stopped                 sleep 60
jan@jan-virtual-machine:/$ fg %1
sleep 60
```

Here the sleep process is created in a subshell, then stopped. Once it is stopped, the *fg* command was used to bring it to the foreground as an active process.

- **wait**: Suspends a script until the running jobs are complete.
  Syntax: *wait process_id*
- disown: Removes a job from shell's active jobs list. If you receive a warning, use the *-a* option.

```
jan@jan-virtual-machine:/$ sleep 60&
[1] 5274
jan@jan-virtual-machine:/$ disown -a %1
jan@jan-virtual-machine:/$ jobs
```

- **stop**: Stops a process. You could simply press **Ctrl+C** as well.
- **Ctrl+Z**: Stops a foreground process.

- **kill**: Kills a process.

```
jan@jan-virtual-machine:/$ sleep 60 &
[2] 5296
[1]    Done                    sleep 60
jan@jan-virtual-machine:/$ jobs
[2]+  Running                  sleep 60 &
jan@jan-virtual-machine:/$ kill %2
jan@jan-virtual-machine:/$ jobs
[2]+  Terminated               sleep 60
```

Linux Environment Variables

Environment variables help define the Linux experience. It serves information to other processes and scripts when requested. It can also be used to temporarily to hold data and configuration.

There are two types of environment variables.

- Global variables.
- Local variables.

Global Variables are available to any shell, as well as spawned child processes. In contrast, local variables are limited to a single shell session. To distinguish, the global environments use capital letters (all caps).

To view the available global environment variables, use the following command.

printenv

```
LANG=en_US.UTF-8
DISPLAY=:0
GNOME_SHELL_SESSION_MODE=ubuntu
COLORTERM=truecolor
USERNAME=jan
XDG_VTNR=2
SSH_AUTH_SOCK=/run/user/1000/keyring/ssh
LC_NAME=en_US.UTF-8
XDG_SESSION_ID=2
USER=jan
DESKTOP_SESSION=ubuntu
QT4_IM_MODULE=xim
TEXTDOMAINDIR=/usr/share/locale/
GNOME_TERMINAL_SCREEN=/org/gnome/Terminal/screen/e3396967_22f5_438e_84a4_30fe231
802ea
PWD=/
HOME=/home/jan
```

As you see there is a huge list. Let's try a few commands and obtain information.

printenv USER

```
jan@jan-virtual-machine:/$ printenv USER
jan
jan@jan-virtual-machine:/$ printenv USERNAME
jan
jan@jan-virtual-machine:/$ printenv PWD
/
jan@jan-virtual-machine:/$ printenv HOSTNAME
jan@jan-virtual-machine:/$ printenv DESKTOP_SESSION
ubuntu
```

echo $HOME

```
jan@jan-virtual-machine:/$ echo $HOME
/home/jan
```

ls $HOME

```
jan@jan-virtual-machine:/$ ls $HOME
Desktop     Downloads          Music      Public      Videos
Documents   examples.desktop_  Pictures   Templates
```

Note: As you see in this example, by passing the variable with a $ sign, it basically allowed it to be passed as a command.

In the next example, we can prove that the global variables return the same when executed in subshells.

```
jan@jan-virtual-machine:/$ echo $HOME
/home/jan
jan@jan-virtual-machine:/$ bash
jan@jan-virtual-machine:/$ $HOME
bash: /home/jan: Is a directory
jan@jan-virtual-machine:/$ ps -f
UID          PID    PPID  C STIME TTY          TIME CMD
jan         4342    4333  0 07:59 pts/0     00:00:00 bash
jan         5193    4342  0 15:50 pts/0     00:00:00 sleep 10
jan         5386    4342  0 17:25 pts/0     00:00:00 bash
jan         5395    5386  0 17:25 pts/0     00:00:00 ps -f
```

As you see with this example, even after running bash the $HOME returns the same value.

When we look into the local variables, those are limited to the local process. The Linux system defines certain standard local variables. A user can define his/her own variables.

There is no command to view these local variables. However, you can use the **set** command to display all the global and local variables. Let's define a variable.

echo $test_variable

test_variable=Jan

echo $test_variable

```
jan@jan-virtual-machine:/$ echo $test_variable

jan@jan-virtual-machine:/$ test_variable=Jan
jan@jan-virtual-machine:/$ echo $test_variable
Jan
```

Proving that local variables only limited to a shell session. In this example, it is local to the subshell spawned by the *bash* command.

```
jan@jan-virtual-machine:/$ bash
jan@jan-virtual-machine:/$ echo $test_1

jan@jan-virtual-machine:/$ test_1="I am local"
jan@jan-virtual-machine:/$ echo $test_1
I am local
jan@jan-virtual-machine:/$ exit
exit
jan@jan-virtual-machine:/$ echo $test_1

jan@jan-virtual-machine:/$ 
```

Tip: To use strings, you must use "". You can also specify numerical values.

Caution: Do not use all caps when you create local variables. Only global variables use this kind of pattern.

Defining a Global Variable

In this example, we are declaring an environment variable using the **export** command. The unset command is also introduced here. It removes a

GLOBAL ="I am a global"

export GLOBAL

echo $ GLOBAL

bash

echo $ GLOBAL

exit

unset GLOBAL

```
jan@jan-virtual-machine:/$ GLOBAL="THIS IS GLOBAL"
jan@jan-virtual-machine:/$ echo $GLOBAL
THIS IS GLOBAL
jan@jan-virtual-machine:/$ export GLOBAL
jan@jan-virtual-machine:/$ bash
jan@jan-virtual-machine:/$ echo $GLOBAL
THIS IS GLOBAL
jan@jan-virtual-machine:/$ exit
exit
jan@jan-virtual-machine:/$ echo $GLOBAL
THIS IS GLOBAL
jan@jan-virtual-machine:/$ unset GLOBAL
jan@jan-virtual-machine:/$ echo $GLOBAL
```

PATH Environment Variable

On any operating system, you must have seen the PATH variable being used. The PATH variable is used when the operating system is requested to execute commands, for instance. It is used to search for and find the program that the command is executed on. We can even modify this variable to fit our need.

To view the current values assigned to it, you now know what command to use.

Echo $PATH

```
jan@jan-virtual-machine:/$ echo $PATH
/usr/local/sbin:/usr/local/bin:/usr/sbin:/usr/bin:/sbin:/bin:/usr/games:/usr/loc
al/games:/snap/bin
```

Setting the PATH Variable to Run Your Script from Your Home Directory

1. Create a basic script in your home folder under your name. Name it *my_script*
2. Enter the following commands to the file and save.
   ps -aux
3. Execute the following command.
   PATH=$PATH:/home/jan/
4. Execute *chmod + my_script*
5. Go to a different directory if required or execute bash and spawn a shell.
6. Run the command *my_script*
7. You will see the *ps -aux* executed and a Windows task manager like list is populating on your terminal.

```
jan@jan-virtual-machine:/$ my_script | head
USER        PID %CPU %MEM    VSZ   RSS TTY      STAT START   TIME COMMAND
root          1  0.0  0.3 159900  6816 ?        Ss   03:04   0:05 /sbin/init spl
ash
root          2  0.0  0.0      0     0 ?        S    03:04   0:00 [kthreadd]
root          3  0.0  0.0      0     0 ?        I<   03:04   0:00 [rcu_gp]
root          4  0.0  0.0      0     0 ?        I<   03:04   0:00 [rcu_par_gp]
root          6  0.0  0.0      0     0 ?        I<   03:04   0:00 [kworker/0:0H-
kb]
root          8  0.0  0.0      0     0 ?        I<   03:04   0:00 [mm_percpu_wq]
root          9  0.0  0.0      0     0 ?        S    03:04   0:06 [ksoftirqd/0]
root         10  0.0  0.0      0     0 ?        I    03:04   0:04 [rcu_sched]
root         11  0.0  0.0      0     0 ?        S    03:04   0:00 [migration/0]
```

Note the | head command. This is to limit the output to 10 lines.

System Variables

Linux operating system uses many environment variables. Upon using the **text mode (login)**, or using an **interactive shell**, or a **non-interactive shell**, bash looks for files for commands. The looked-up files depend on the method aforementioned.

When you log into a Linux operating system, bash shell loads as a login shell. This login shell looks for 5 different files for commands. Those are,

- /etc/profile
- $HOME/.bash_profile
- $HOME/.bashrc
- $HOME/.bash_login
- $HOME/.profile

/etc/profile

The uppermost one is the default startup file for bash shell. Upon login bash executes the commands in /etc/profile. Let's look at the content of this file on Ubuntu.

```
jan@jan-virtual-machine:/$ cat /etc/profile
# /etc/profile: system-wide .profile file for the Bourne shell (sh(1))
# and Bourne compatible shells (bash(1), ksh(1), ash(1), ...).

if [ "${PS1-}" ]; then
  if [ "${BASH-}" ] && [ "$BASH" != "/bin/sh" ]; then
    # The file bash.bashrc already sets the default PS1.
    # PS1='\h:\w\$ '
    if [ -f /etc/bash.bashrc ]; then
      . /etc/bash.bashrc
    fi
  else
    if [ "`id -u`" -eq 0 ]; then
      PS1='# '
    else
      PS1='$ '
    fi
  fi
fi

if [ -d /etc/profile.d ]; then
  for i in /etc/profile.d/*.sh; do
    if [ -r $i ]; then
      . $i
    fi
  done
  unset i
fi
```

Here, you can see the invoke of /etc/bash.bashrc. As we discussed before, this contains system environment variables. You should have also noticed /etc/profile.d. This hosts application specific startup files. These files are executed when you log into the shell. Let's look at the files.

Command: *ls- l /etc/profile.d*

```
jan@jan-virtual-machine:~/Desktop$ ls -l /etc/profile.d/
total 28
-rw-r--r-- 1 root root   96 Aug 20  2018 01-locale-fix.sh
-rw-r--r-- 1 root root  825 Jun  5 12:11 apps-bin-path.sh
-rw-r--r-- 1 root root  664 Apr  2  2018 bash_completion.sh
-rw-r--r-- 1 root root 1003 Dec 29  2015 cedilla-portuguese.sh
-rw-r--r-- 1 root root  652 Apr  3 22:37 input-method-config.sh
-rw-r--r-- 1 root root 1941 Jul 16  2018 vte-2.91.sh
-rw-r--r-- 1 root root  954 May  2  2018 xdg_dirs_desktop_session.sh
```

$HOME

As you already detected the rest except /etc/profile has this in common. The purpose is to provide user-specific startup files to define user-specific variables. There is a '.' next to each and it denotes a hidden file.

Interactive Shell

Interactive shell is started when you start the bash shell without login into a system. Although this does not act like the login shell, it still accepts commands.

If interactive shell is started, it does not need to process the /etc/profile. It directly looks for .bashrc file in the HOME directory of the user. This first looks for a common *bashrc* file in the /etc directory. Then it provides a place for the user to input personal command aliases and private scripts.

Non-interactive Shell

In this case, the system starts to execute a shell script, although this does not require any interaction, it is required to run startup commands each time a script is started. This is where a special global environment variable comes into play. This is called BASH_ENV.

Command: echo $BASH_ENV

```
jan@jan-virtual-machine:/home$ echo $BASH_ENV

jan@jan-virtual-machine:/home$ █
```

As you notice there is nothing set. Then how does it work?

If you can recall, some commands spawn a subshell and this child shell inherits parent's exported variables.

As you are aware, if a script does not spawn a subshell, the variables are already available in the current shell environment. Now even if BASH_ENV is not set, the local and global variables for the current shell is already available.

Using Permanent or Persistent Environment Variables

When you create environment variables, especially for your needs, you must store these in a permanent location. You might think /etc/profile is the best place for storing the global variables, but it isn't. It can change things upon system activities, such as upgrades. Instead,

/etc/profile.d can be utilized to store *.sh* files. For local variables, the best place would be the .bashrc file in the HOME directory of the user.

Finally, we will discuss some details about the variable arrays.

Variable Arrays

Environment variables can be used as arrays. This is a great feature of environment variables. If you do not know what an array is, an array is a place in memory (a variable) that can store multiple values. Let's look at an example.

va_months=(Jan, Feb, Mar, Apr, May, Jun, Jul, Aug, Sep, Oct, Nov, Dec)

echo $va_months

echo ${va_months[0]}

The first command creates the array and assigns the values. The second echoes the first element of the array. The third echoes the same. We can also modify an array item by using the following command (example).

va_months[0]=January

echo ${va_months[0]}

Finally, to display all the array elements, use the '*'.

echo ${va_months[*]}


```
jan@jan-virtual-machine:/home$ va_months=(Jan, Feb, Mar, Apr, May, Jun, Jul, Aug
, Sep, Oct, Nov, Dec)
jan@jan-virtual-machine:/home$ echo $va_months
Jan,
jan@jan-virtual-machine:/home$ echo ${va_months[0]}
Jan,
jan@jan-virtual-machine:/home$ echo ${va_months[1]}
Feb,
jan@jan-virtual-machine:/home$ echo ${va_months[11]}
Dec
jan@jan-virtual-machine:/home$ echo ${va_months[*]}
Jan, Feb, Mar, Apr, May, Jun, Jul, Aug, Sep, Oct, Nov, Dec
jan@jan-virtual-machine:/home$ va_months[0]=January
jan@jan-virtual-machine:/home$ echo ${va_months[0]}
January
```

CHAPTER 8: Building Scripts

In this chapter you will learn

> Writing Shell scripts
>
> Command aliases and substitutions
>
> Pipes
>
> Files, Descriptors and exit status
>
> Structured commands (if, for, while, until, break, continue).

In this chapter, you are going to gain a comprehensive understanding of script building with examples. The key to script building is your familiarity with commands. Scripting is highly advantageous, as it can process more than one command, process the results, and feed one result to the other building a chain.

You already know how to execute multiple commands using ';'. For instance, pwd; cd ..; is a combination. What is it? It is a basic shell script!

Writing Shell Scripts

To write a shell script you simply need some understanding of Linux commands and a text editor. On Ubuntu, the default editor can be used (gedit). Let's examine the components.

A shell script starts with a comment at the top.

#!/bin/shell_type

For instance, *#!/bin/bash*

This is a comment as it starts with the '#'. These lines are not interpreted by the shell! To comment, '#' should be used. However, this specific line tells the shell what shell to use to execute this script on. We call #! **Shebang**.

The next part will be a set of commands with explanations. If you are familiar with programming, shell scripting is similar.

If we create a script with the following example,

#!/bin/bash

who

#who command displays the account you are currently logged into and at what #time the user logged into the system.

pwd

it should work as expected.

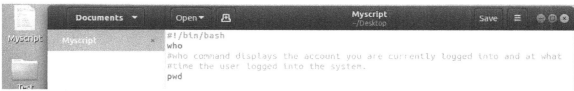

Image: who command in a script

> **Note**: A file which starts with the comment at the top designates the file as a script. Also notice the color changes.

However, you have to either place it in the /bin directory or you have to use the PATH variable, as instructed in the previous chapter, to set the path to your directory. You could also use the absolute or relative path.

The next thing you need to do is the changing of permissions. Why? Let's create a file and examine the permissions.

```
jan@jan-virtual-machine:~/Desktop$ ls -l Myscript
-rw-r--r-- 1 jan jan 137 Sep 23 17:29 Myscript
```

According to the result, there is insufficient permissions to execute this file. The system treats itself as a script, but it hasn't modified the permissions. It is up to the user.

To provide execution permissions, *chmod* command can be used.

chmod u+x Myscript

```
jan@jan-virtual-machine:~/Desktop$ ls -l Myscript
-rwxr--r-- 1 jan jan 137 Sep 23 17:29 Myscript
```

Once this step is complete, the script is ready to be executed.

```
jan@jan-virtual-machine:~/Desktop$ ./Myscript
jan      :0              2019-09-21 05:09 (:0)
/home/jan/Desktop
```

If you want to display text guides, the output of environment variables and such, you can use the echo command. We have learned environment variables in a previous lesson.

Command Aliases

Using a command alias can save a lot of time. To define an alias, you have to do a simple assignment.

Syntax: alias=command(s)

Examples:

- *alias L="ls -al"*
- *alias search=grep*

Command Substitution

It is also possible to use an output of a command as an input to a variable. This is a great feature to continue the script and execute with dynamic data.

To achieve this, you must use $().

Example: *user_name=$(USERNAME)*

Example Script:

#!/bin/bash

user_name=$(who)

echo "Your username is :" $user_name

```
jan@jan-virtual-machine:~/Desktop$ ./Myscript
"Your username is :" jan :0 2019-09-24 03:42 (:0)
```

Creating Files

Another great feature is that you can output the results. You can even name the file according to your needs. This is explained in the next example.

#!/bin/bash

mydate=$(date +%Y%m%d)

echo "Today is :" $mydate

who > log.$mydate

ls -l log.$mydate

```
jan@jan-virtual-machine:~/Desktop$ ./Myscript
"Today is :" 20190924
-rw-r--r-- 1 jan jan 44 Sep 24 06:19 log.20190924
```

Here, we create a date and format it. %Y is the year in YYYY format. The month is in numeric format (e.g., 09) and the date is in numeric format as well. The output is similar to YYYYMMDD. The output is taken into a variable. Then we echo the variable. Finally, we use the who command and **redirect** it's input to a new file using the redirect operator >. The file name is created as the "log".YYYYMMDD. This is how we create logs to keep records. If the script runs on next day, the filename will be log.20190925.

Redirection is an extremely useful feature. Instead of using commands like *touch*, you can redirect the output to a file. Yet, you can even create files from scripts by using the *touch* command. For instance,

#!/bin/bash

mydate=$(date +%Y%m%d)

echo "Today is :" $mydate

touch log.$mydate   #Creates a file and name the first part .lo and later using #our variable

who >> log.$mydate   #Append the output of 'who' command to the file.

```
jan@jan-virtual-machine:~/Desktop$ ./Myscript
"Today is :" 20190924
jan@jan-virtual-machine:~/Desktop$ ls -al log.20190924
-rw-r--r-- 1 jan jan 44 Sep 24 06:29 log.20190924
jan@jan-virtual-machine:~/Desktop$ cat log.20190924
jan      :0                 2019-09-24 03:42 (:0)
```

Tip: The **>>** operator is used to append entries to a file. This is an extremely useful command.

You can also do the reverse the process we performed using the '>' operator. This is known as **input redirection**. For instance, we could get an entry of a file to a new variable or a command directly. The following example explains this in detail.

#!/bin/bash

wc < log.20190924

 # wc is a new command to you. It counts the number of lines, words and #characters.

```
jan@jan-virtual-machine:~/Desktop$ ./Myscript
 1  5 44
```

Finally, we will look into the '<<' operator. This is known as the **inline input operator**.

Example: *wc << lastLine*

```
jan@jan-virtual-machine:~/Desktop$ wc << lastLine
> test
> test2
> test3
> lastLine
 3  3 17
```

As you notice, until the *lastLine* was entered as text input, it captured the user input.

Other examples:

Redirecting error and standard output to the same file. You could use the following command.

Example: *ls Test Test2 Test3> dirlist 2>&1*

Here, we are trying to list the properties of the Test directory. Remember, *ls* command supports multiple file or directory names. It then lists each file's or directory's properties. *Test* and *Test2* directories are on my desktop. *Test3* directory does not exist. I am redirecting the output of this command as well as the error into a new file called *dirlist*.

```
jan@jan-virtual-machine:~/Desktop$ ls Test Test2 Test3> dirlist 2>&1
jan@jan-virtual-machine:~/Desktop$ cat dirlist
ls: cannot access 'Test3': No such file or directory
Test:
File5.txt

Test2:
File6.txt
```

Standard File Descriptors

We are revisiting the file descriptors again.

Standard Input - 0: STDIN

Standard Output – 1: STDOUT

Standard Error - 2: STDERR

The first is standard input, the next are standard output and standard error. The numerical values are file descriptors.

In addition to these techniques, pipes are extensively used in scripts.

Pipes

Piping is useful when an output of a command is required as an input of another. This is something we have learned so far. The operator used is '|'.

Example:

#!/bin/bash

cat employee.txt | sort -nr -k 2

#Here we redirect the file entry we obtain to the sort function. It sorts by numeric #values, in reverse order and sort by column id (2nd column).

```
jan@jan-virtual-machine:~/Desktop$ ./Myscript
Jake      20000
Ruth      15000
K.D.      12500
Dan       12000
Jan       3000
```

Mathematical Operations in Script Building

Any script can be used to perform certain calculations. There are some built-in commands in Linux. We are looking into the command **expr**. This stands for the expression. These are the operators for *expr* command.

```
ARG1 | ARG2          ARG1 if it is neither null nor 0, otherwise ARG2

ARG1 & ARG2          ARG1 if neither argument is null or 0, otherwise 0

ARG1 < ARG2          ARG1 is less than ARG2
ARG1 <= ARG2         ARG1 is less than or equal to ARG2
ARG1 = ARG2          ARG1 is equal to ARG2
ARG1 != ARG2         ARG1 is unequal to ARG2
ARG1 >= ARG2         ARG1 is greater than or equal to ARG2
ARG1 > ARG2          ARG1 is greater than ARG2

ARG1 + ARG2          arithmetic sum of ARG1 and ARG2
ARG1 - ARG2          arithmetic difference of ARG1 and ARG2

ARG1 * ARG2          arithmetic product of ARG1 and ARG2
ARG1 / ARG2          arithmetic quotient of ARG1 divided by ARG2
ARG1 % ARG2          arithmetic remainder of ARG1 divided by ARG2

STRING : REGEXP      anchored pattern match of REGEXP in STRING

match STRING REGEXP       same as STRING : REGEXP
substr STRING POS LENGTH  substring of STRING, POS counted from 1
index STRING CHARS        index in STRING where any CHARS is found, or 0
length STRING             length of STRING
+ TOKEN                   interpret TOKEN as a string, even if it is a
                             keyword like 'match' or an operator like '/'

( EXPRESSION )            value of EXPRESSION
```

Image: expr operators

Examples:

```
jan@jan-virtual-machine:~/Desktop$ expr 1+1
1+1
jan@jan-virtual-machine:~/Desktop$ expr 1 + 1
2
jan@jan-virtual-machine:~/Desktop$ expr 2 - 1
1
jan@jan-virtual-machine:~/Desktop$ expr 2 * 2
expr: syntax error
jan@jan-virtual-machine:~/Desktop$ expr 2 \* 2
4
jan@jan-virtual-machine:~/Desktop$ expr 6 / 3
2
```

Rather than using the expr command, it is more convenient to use brackets.

#!/bin/bash

var1=2

var2=6

var3=3

var4=$(expr $var1 * $var2)

echo $var4

*var5=$[($var1 * $var2)/$var3]*

echo $var5

```
jan@jan-virtual-machine:~/Desktop$ ./Myscript
12
4
```

The Bash Calculator

When you want to perform more complex mathematical functions, there is a built-in bash tool to perform this. It is the **bash calculator**. The command is *bc*.

```
jan@jan-virtual-machine:~/Desktop$ bc
bc 1.07.1
Copyright 1991-1994, 1997, 1998, 2000, 2004, 2006, 2008, 2012-2017 Free Software
 Foundation, Inc.
This is free software with ABSOLUTELY NO WARRANTY.
For details type `warranty'.
quit
```

Tip: To exit from this tool, type *quit* and press enter. While in bc, you can perform math operations.

The bash calculator supports the following.

- Numerical values (integer and floating-point numbers).
- Variables.
- Expressions.
- Functions.
- Statements (i.e., if-then-else).
- Comments.

```
jan@jan-virtual-machine:~/Desktop$ bc
bc 1.07.1
Copyright 1991-1994, 1997, 1998, 2000, 2004, 2006, 2008, 2012-2017 Free Software
 Foundation, Inc.
This is free software with ABSOLUTELY NO WARRANTY.
For details type `warranty'.
1 * 4
4
1.56 * 2
3.12
1.2222*2
2.4444
8.45/5
1
```

In the last line, you can see a problem. $8.45/5 = 1$. This is inaccurate unless it is rounded up. The problem here is the number of decimal places. It is handled by a built-in variable known as *scale*. To receive the intended output, we need to modify the scale.

```
jan@jan-virtual-machine:~/Desktop$ bc
bc 1.07.1
Copyright 1991-1994, 1997, 1998, 2000, 2004, 2006, 2008, 2012-2017 Free Software
 Foundation, Inc.
This is free software with ABSOLUTELY NO WARRANTY.
For details type `warranty'.
scale=5
8.45/5
1.69000
```

Tip: To remove the description you get with *bc*, use the **-q** option.

The *bc* command supports variables. The following example uses variables instead of numerical values.

```
jan@jan-virtual-machine:~/Desktop$ bc -q
var1=10
var2=5
var3=var1/var2
var3
2
```

The next important task is to get *bc* working in a script. In this case, we need to depend on pipes.

```
#!/bin/bash

var1=10

var2=2

var3=$(echo "$var1 ^ $var2" | bc)

echo "The answer is: "$var3
```

```
jan@jan-virtual-machine:~/Desktop$ ./Myscript
The answer is: 100
```

Another example using the *scale* option.

```
#!/bin/bash

var1=10

var2=3

var3=$(echo " scale=3; $var1 / $var2" | bc)

echo "The answer is: "$var3
```

```
jan@jan-virtual-machine:~/Desktop$ ./Myscript
The answer is: 3.333
```

The next example will be looking into how the inline input operator can be used with the *bc* command in a script.

```
#!/bin/bash

var1=8

var2=1.75

var3=3

varF=$(bc << EOF # EOF stands for End of File

scale = 4

v1 = ( $var1 * $var2)
```

v2 = ($var1 / $var3)

v1 + v2

EOF

)

echo The final calculation is: $varF

```
jan@jan-virtual-machine:~/Desktop$ ./Myscript
The final calculation is: 16.6666
```

Exit Status

It is always good to check the exist status of a command, executable, or a script to verify if there were any problems at the end of the execution. This is good for debugging and to maintain stability. There is a special operator **'$?'**.

Example: Let's execute our previous script. Before, we need to add a line to the end of the script.

echo $?

```
jan@jan-virtual-machine:~/Desktop$ ./Myscript
The final calculation is: 16.6666
0
```

Once the script is executed, the exist status is 0. This indicates a successful completion. Let's introduce an error.

#!/bin/bash

ls -la Test3

echo $?

Remember, there is no Test3 directory on my desktop.

```
jan@jan-virtual-machine:~/Desktop$ ./Myscript
ls: cannot access 'Test3': No such file or directory
2
```

Now let's execute a script with a fake command.

#!/bin/bash

a

echo $?

```
jan@jan-virtual-machine:~/Desktop$ ./Myscript
./Myscript: line 2: a: command not found
127
```

Let's examine the exit codes. The following tables lists the exit codes and their meaning.

Table 8.1: Exit codes

Code	Meaning
0	Command completed successfully
1	Unknown error
2	Misuse of the command
126	The command cannot be executed
127	Command not found
128	
128+x	
130	
225	

There is a more interesting feature of the exist status. It is that you can define your own exit codes. This is achieved with the command exit followed by a numeric value specified by you.

Example:

#!/bin/bash

ls -la Test

exit 100

```
jan@jan-virtual-machine:~/Desktop$ ./Myscript
total 12
drwxr-xr-t 2 jan jan 4096 Sep 21 22:12 .
drwxr-xr-x 4 jan jan 4096 Sep 24 12:39 ..
-rw-rw-r-- 1 jan jan   60 Sep 21 07:26 File5.txt
jan@jan-virtual-machine:~/Desktop$ echo $?
100
```

At the end of the results, when the echo $? was executed, it displays our exit code.

Another example:

#!/bin/bash

ls -la Test

echo $?

exit 100

```
jan@jan-virtual-machine:~/Desktop$ ./Myscript
total 12
drwxr-xr-t 2 jan jan 4096 Sep 21 22:12 .
drwxr-xr-x 4 jan jan 4096 Sep 24 12:42 ..
-rw-rw-r-- 1 jan jan   60 Sep 21 07:26 File5.txt
0
jan@jan-virtual-machine:~/Desktop$ echo $?
100
jan@jan-virtual-machine:~/Desktop$
```

If you look at the exit codes, it is possible to identify a range (0 – 255). It is because the shell is calculating the exit code using a method called modulo arithmetic. It divides the error by 256 and use the remainder as the exit code.

Structured Commands

Until now we have learned a lot of commands and how to build basic scripts. You can also use man command or --help option to learn many things about the commands and other features.

For scripting, if you are programmer or even a newbie, you must apply some condition. Otherwise, we cannot build structures of commands to obtain a logical output when we are to build scripts to apply real-life scenarios that may require more complex logic.

To resolve this the scripts can utilize structured commands like if-then-else and for just like in other programming languages. These are called conditionals or logical structures. In this section, we are going to learn the structured commands in depth. Let's start with a simple one first.

if-then-fi and if-then-else-fi

In any programing language and logic, if-then logic is the most fundamental. You can use the same in scripting. The following is how this can be used.

if [expression];

then

code if 'expression' is true.

Fi

> **Note**: Now here we are using a [] but it is not required. If we use [] we are using a **test condition**. Let's take an example without []

```
#!/bin/bash
if grep APR --color File3.txt
then
        echo "APR is found in the file"
else
        echo "APR is not found"
fi
```

```
jan@jan-virtual-machine:~/Desktop$ ./Myscript
APR
APR
APR is found in the file
```

However, this method is not effective if we cannot do comparisons. For instance, if you are willing to compare more than one case e.g., APR, MAY, JUN etc. and do some logical operations, you need a technique to do so. This is when the test feature comes into play.

if test condition

then

commands

fi

Without using the word test, we can simply use square brackets. When you do, you must be careful of a few things.

-   You must keep a space from the left-most bracket.
-   You must keep a space from the right-most bracket.

The test condition can compare numeric values, strings and files. Let's also learn what the operators and how to use them.

-   **eq**: The equal to operator is used to compare 2 values.
-   **le**: Less than or equal to operator.
-   **lt**: Less than operator.
-   **ge**: Greater than or equal to operator.
-   **gt**: Greater than operator.
-   **ne**: Not equals operator.

We can also use string comparisons in a similar method. The operators are as follows.

-   **str1 = str2**: Matches 2 strings for equality.
-   **str1 != str2**: Matches for inequality.
-   **str1 > str2**: Greater than operator.
-   **str1 < str2**: Less than operator.
-   **-z** str1: Checks for 0 length.
-   **-n** str1: Checks for a length more than 0.

Let's also look at the file comparison operators.

Table: File comparison operators

Operator	Description
FILE1 -ef FILE2	FILE1 and FILE2 have the same device and **inode** numbers
FILE1 -nt FILE2	FILE1 is newer (modification date) than FILE2
FILE1 -ot FILE2	FILE1 is older than FILE2
-b FILE	FILE exists and is block special
-c FILE	FILE exists and is character special
-d FILE	FILE exists and is a directory
-e FILE	FILE exists
-f FILE	FILE exists and is a regular file
-g FILE	FILE exists and is set-group-ID
-G FILE	FILE exists and is owned by the effective group ID
-h FILE	FILE exists and is a symbolic link (same as -L)
-k FILE	FILE exists and has its sticky bit set
-L FILE	FILE exists and is a symbolic link (same as -h)
-O FILE	FILE exists and is owned by the effective user ID
-p FILE	FILE exists and is a named pipe
-r FILE	FILE exists and read permission is granted
-s FILE	FILE exists and has a size greater than zero
-S FILE	FILE exists and is a socket

-t FD	File descriptor FD is opened on a terminal
-u FILE	FILE exists and its set-user-ID bit is set
-w FILE	FILE exists and write permission is granted
-x FILE	FILE exists and execute (or search) permission is granted

Let's look at some examples.

Example:

#!/bin/bash

T1="Jan"

T2="Jake"

if ["$T1" = "$T2"]; then

echo true

else

echo false

fi

```
jan@jan-virtual-machine:~/Desktop$ ./Myscript
false
```

In this example we match two strings. Using if we match the commands in order to obtain whether the match is true or false. This logic is called Boolean logic.

What happens if we put commands before and after the if statement? Well, these will not be considered as parts of the if statement! They will be executed or failed accordingly outside the statement.

In this command, we use an *else* to match the error condition. That is if the matching results in a failure. If you remove the else and the echo false, what will be the result?

Example:

T1="Jan"

T2="Jake"

if ["$T1" = "$T2"]; then

echo true

fi

```
jan@jan-virtual-machine:~/Desktop$ ./Myscript
jan@jan-virtual-machine:~/Desktop$ 
```

As you notice, there is no output. Because, it simply jumped out of the if statement since the two names do not match. In this example, we use the logical operator '='. We could use '!=' to evaluate a mismatch instead (or *-ne*). The '!' applies the NOT logic. In conjunction with the EQUAL operator, the logic is 'NOT EQUAL'. If T1 is not equal to T2, then return true.

if ["$T1" != "$T2"]; then

```
jan@jan-virtual-machine:~/Desktop$ ./Myscript
true
```

You can specify more actions between *if [expression]; then* and *fi*.

Let's match an exit code in this example and add more commands in between.

#!/bin/bash

varx=$(ls -l Test 2>/dev/null)$?

echo $varx

if [$varx -eq 0]; then

      echo A match found

      echo varx?

else   echo "The file/directory does not exist"

fi

In this example, we are getting an output of the ls command's exit code. If the directory exists, the exit code will be 0. If the directory does not exist, it will be something else (1). We are suppressing the error message by sending it o /dev/null. At the end of the expression we request the exist code.

Then we are outputting the exit code by using echo command. Finally, we are comparing the exit code. If it is o, then there is a match, and we echo varx again.

If the exit code does not match, then **else** is true and the other message will be displayed (The file/directory does not exist). Why we need else here? To match the **false** logic. In a longer form we will be using **elif** (else if) to match cases.

```
jan@jan-virtual-machine:~/Desktop$ ./Myscript
0
A match found
0
```

As you see the directory existed and the return code is o. Let's remove the directory and try again.

```
jan@jan-virtual-machine:~/Desktop$ ./Myscript
2
The file/directory does not exist
```

Now the directory is gone, and the output is as expected.

Using Nested If

In a script you may need to match more than Boolean logic. Instead, you may have to match each and every case. For example, if you run the ls command, there can be more exit codes to match and upon each code, we can take action. This method is called nesting. Let's look at an example.

#!/bin/bash

a=10

b=20

if [$a -eq $b]

then

   echo "a = b"

elif [$a -gt $b]

then

```
  echo "a > b"
elif [ $a -lt $b ]
then
  echo "a < b"
else
  echo "None of the conditions have met"
fi
```

```
jan@jan-virtual-machine:~/Desktop$ ./Myscript
a < b
```

The output is accurate and as expected.

Let's try another example.

```
#!/bin/bash
user_name=jake
if grep $user_name /etc/passwd
then
echo "The user $user_name found in the system."
elif ls -d /home/$user_name
then
echo "The user $user_name not found but a profile directory exists"
fi
```

```
jan@jan-virtual-machine:~/Desktop$ ./Myscript
jake:x:1001:1001:Jake,,,:/home/jake:/bin/bash
The user jake found in the system.
```

Let's delete the user now without removing his files.

```
jan@jan-virtual-machine:~/Desktop$ su -
Password:
root@jan-virtual-machine:~# userdel jake
root@jan-virtual-machine:~# su jan
```

Now, let's execute the script again.

```
jan@jan-virtual-machine:~/Desktop$ ./Myscript
/home/jake
The user jake not found but a profile directory exists
```

Since we have not used the **-f** option with *userdel*, the profile folder existed. This is a useful way to find remaining files when you delete a user.

We can even extend this code by adding another case. Let's look at the following example. This time the home directory of *jake* has been removed.

#!/bin/bash

user_name=jake

if grep $user_name /etc/passwd

then

echo "The user $user_name found in the system."

elif ls -d /home/$user_name

then

echo "The user $user_name not found but a profile directory exists"

else

      echo "The user $user_name does not exist!"

fi

```
jan@jan-virtual-machine:~/Desktop$ ./Myscript
ls: cannot access '/home/jake': No such file or directory
"The user jake does not exist!"
```

Now, let's look at some file comparison examples.

#!/bin/bash

mydir=$/home/jan

if [-d mydir]

then

    echo "The directory $mydir exists!"

    ls -l $mydir

else

    echo "The directory $mydir does not exist"

fi

```
jan@jan-virtual-machine:~/Desktop$ ./Myscript
"The directory /home/jan exists!"
total 48
drwxr-xr-x 3 jan jan 4096 ಐಔಥ್ 24 17:27 Desktop
drwxr-xr-x 3 jan jan 4096 ಐಔಥ್ 18 10:54 Documents
drwxr-xr-x 2 jan jan 4096 ಐಔಥ್ 17 04:37 Downloads
-rw-r--r-- 1 jan jan 8980 ಐಔಥ್ 17 04:24 examples.desktop
drwxr-xr-x 2 jan jan 4096 ಐಔಥ್ 17 04:37 Music
-rwxrwxr-x 1 jan jan   10 ಐಔಥ್ 22 19:12 my_script
drwxr-xr-x 2 jan jan 4096 ಐಔಥ್ 17 13:05 Pictures
drwxr-xr-x 2 jan jan 4096 ಐಔಥ್ 17 04:37 Public
drwxr-xr-x 2 jan jan 4096 ಐಔಥ್ 17 04:37 Templates
drwxr-xr-x 2 jan jan 4096 ಐಔಥ್ 17 04:37 Videos
```

Let's now compare the date of two files and append some text from the newer (temp) file if the other file is older.

#!/bin/bash

varF=/home/jan/Desktop/File1.txt

ls -al > temp.txt

if [temp.txt -nt File1.txt]

then

    temp.txt >> File1.txt

    echo File updated

else

    echo The file is newer than the temporary file

fi

```
jan@jan-virtual-machine:~/Desktop$ cat File1.txt
This has only one line.
jan@jan-virtual-machine:~/Desktop$ ./Myscript
File updated
jan@jan-virtual-machine:~/Desktop$ cat File1.txt
This has only one line.
total 52
drwxr-xr-x  3 jan jan 4096 송쪽  24 17:37 .
drwxr-xr-x 18 jan jan 4096 송쪽  24 03:42 ..
-rw-r--r--  1 jan jan  770 송쪽  23 14:45 archive.tar.gz
-rw-r--r--  1 jan jan   87 송쪽  24 06:58 dirlist
-rw-rw-r--  1 jan jan   52 송쪽  24 07:06 employee.txt
-rw-rw-r--  1 jan jan  242 송쪽  22 23:56 File11.txt.bz2
-rw-r--r--  1 jan jan   24 송쪽  24 17:35 File1.txt
-rw-rw-r--  1 jan jan  242 송쪽  23 00:12 File1.txt.bz2
-rw-r--r--  1 jan jan   24 송쪽  21 22:10 File3.txt
-rw-r--r--  1 jan jan   44 송쪽  24 06:19 log.
-rw-r--r--  1 jan jan   44 송쪽  24 06:29 log.20190924
-rwxr--r--  1 jan jan  197 송쪽  24 17:37 Myscript
-rw-rw-r--  1 jan jan    0 송쪽  24 17:37 temp.txt
drwxrwxr-x  2 jan jan 4096 송쪽  21 22:12 Test2
```

We can also use this method to know if you can read a file, write to a file, update log files, and add dates to logs with other details in real-life scenarios. Let's try if we can verify a file exists and if we can write to it.

file_name=/home/jan/Desktop/myfile

if [-f $file_name] #If the file is a file and exists

then

if [-s $file_name] #If the file size is greater than zero

then

    if [-w $file_name]

    then

        echo "This file is writable"

        date >> $file_name

    else

        echo "This file is not writable!"

    fi

else

    "echo This file is empty"

fi

else

```
jan@jan-virtual-machine:~/Desktop$ ./Myscript
This file is writable
jan@jan-virtual-machine:~/Desktop$
jan@jan-virtual-machine:~/Desktop$ chmod u-w myfile
jan@jan-virtual-machine:~/Desktop$ ./Myscript
This file is not writable!
jan@jan-virtual-machine:~/Desktop$ rm -i myfile
rm: remove write-protected regular file 'myfile'? y
jan@jan-virtual-machine:~/Desktop$ ./Myscript
No such file exists!
```

We are testing each branch, and this is the output when the file is there, when the file is not writable, and finally when it is removed or does not exist.

Combining Test Cases with Boolean Operators

When you write scripts, you may need to compare more than one test cases (complex cases) for decision making. There are two operators '**&&**' and '**||**' representing 'AND' and 'OR' logic. For instance, we could match if a file exists and if the size is zero.

Example: *if [-f filename.txt] && [-s filename.txt]*

Using Even More Features

There are several other advanced features, such as double parentheses and double square brackets, used for mathematical operations and advanced string operations.

We used double parentheses also to use internal operations rather than letting the single parenthesis to spawn subshells.

There are several symbols you need to understand before you proceed.

Table 8.3: Logical operators

Symbol	Description
!	Logical negation
~	Bitwise negation
&	Bitwise AND
&&	Logical AND
|	Bitwise OR
||	Logical OR
**	Exponentiation
--val	Pre-decrement
val--	Post-decrement
++val	Pre-increment
val++	Post-increment
<<	Bitwise-shift (Left)

>>	Bitwise-shift (Right)

The Case Command

The **case** command is extremely useful when there is a long ladder of if-then-else statements. With the case command, the stages can be represented as cases.

Syntax:

case $variable-name in

      pattern1)

            command1

    ...

      commandN

    ;;

      patternN)

            command1

    ...

      commandN

    ;;

    *)

   esac

You can also use *pattern1|pattern2|pattern3)* to match multiple patterns instead of a single pattern. Case command can be used for highly advanced decision-making constructs.

Advanced example:

#!/bin/bash

if [-z $1] #if the script runs without argument

then

  rental="Unknown vehicle"

elif [-n $1]

then

 # If supplied make first argument as a rental

  rental=$1

fi

 # use case statement for rental decision making

case $rental in

    "car") echo "For $rental rental is $25 per k/m.";;

    "van") echo "For $rental rental is$20 per k/m.";;

    "jeep") echo "For $rental rental is $18 per k/m.";;

    "bicycle") echo "For $rental rental $1 per k/m.";;

    *) echo "Sorry, no $rental rental is available for you!";;

esac

Executing this script is somewhat different from the previous scripts. To execute this, you must provide an argument with the execution command.

```
jan@jan-virtual-machine:~/Desktop$ ./Myscript car
For car rental is 5 per k/m.
jan@jan-virtual-machine:~/Desktop$ ./Myscript
Sorry, no Unknown vehicle rental is available for you!
jan@jan-virtual-machine:~/Desktop$ ./Myscript j
Sorry, no j rental is available for you!
```

Another example:

#!/bin/bash

```
case $USER in

root)

        echo "Welcome Superuser";;

jan | jake)

        echo "Welcome administrator!";;

testuser)

        echo "Welcome test! Please use the dev board for reporting";;

*)

        echo "Access is denied!";;

esac
```

```
jan@jan-virtual-machine:~/Desktop$ ./Myscript
Welcome administrator!
jan@jan-virtual-machine:~/Desktop$ su -
Password:
root@jan-virtual-machine:~# /home/jan/Desktop/Myscript
Welcome Superuser
```

The for Command

In scripting, you will often find requirements for command iteration or looping. For instance, when you read from a file or a set of files this becomes remarkably useful.

Syntax:

for var in list

do

commands

done

Here, *var* variable holds the current list item value. At the end of a full iteration it holds the value of the last iteration.

Basic example

#!/bin/bash

for i in {1..5}

do

  echo "Welcome $i times"

done

```
jan@jan-virtual-machine:~/Desktop$ ./Myscript
Welcome 1 times
Welcome 2 times
Welcome 3 times
Welcome 4 times
Welcome 5 times
```

For command can be used in the following method. This is mostly used in programming.

C-style Commands

The following syntax is known as the C-style. In C programming language, such expression style is used for loops etc.

Syntax:

for ((EXP1; EXP2; EXP3))

do

     command1

     command2

     command3

done

Example:

#!/bin/bash

for ((a=0; a<=5; a++))

do

  echo "Welcome $a times"

done

```
jan@jan-virtual-machine:~/Desktop$ ./Myscript
Welcome 0 times
Welcome 1 times
Welcome 2 times
Welcome 3 times
Welcome 4 times
Welcome 5 times
```

We can even utilize multiple expressions. For instance, we could use the following.

for ((a=0, b=9; a<=5; a++,b--))

For with IF command

It is possible to combine for with if in order to exit loops when a condition is met. There are other uses as well. For instance, when you want to find a file, you could search for the file name using a for loop. By using if you can end the loop when the file is found.

Advanced example:

#!/bin/bash

for file in /etc/*

do

      if ["${file}" == "/etc/resolv.conf"]

      then

```
            countNameservers=$(grep -c nameserver /etc/resolv.conf)

            line=$(grep -n nameserver /etc/resolv.conf)

            lineNumber=${line%:*}

            echo "Total  ${countNameservers} nameservers defined in ${file}"

            head -n $lineNumber /etc/resolv.conf | tail -1

            #echo $varRes

            break

      fi
done
```

This example is a complex one. It searches for the name resolution table (file). When it is found, it counts the nameservers and echoes the count. It also displays a nameserver list by taking line number to the line variable and then obtaining the line number out of a string (this string has the line number before the ':'). Then we use head and tail commands to display the entries.

> **Note**: The nameserver file often have more than one entry. If this is true, the script may not work as it still requires another loop to iterate through the list.

When you use for loop, remember not to use certain expressions such as strings with ' symbol. It can mess up the output. Do not also use multi-word values in strings as *for* command will assume each list item is separated by a space. If you use New Name as a single list item, it will treat as two. You need to use "" as appropriate.

As you previously did, you could read list from a variable. For instance,

```
#!/bin/bash

list="Car Bus Bike Helicopter"

for vehicle in $list

do

echo "Have you ever traveled back home by $vehicle?"
```

done

```
jan@jan-virtual-machine:~/Desktop$ ./Myscript
Have you ever traveled back home by Car?
Have you ever traveled back home by Bus?
Have you ever traveled back home by Bike?
Have you ever traveled back home by Helicopter?
```

It can also be used to read values from a command.

Example: In this example, we are using a file with a list of vehicles.

#!/bin/bash

list="vehicles"

for vehicle in $(cat $list)

do

echo "Travel home by $vehicle"

done

```
jan@jan-virtual-machine:~/Desktop$ ./Myscript
Travel home by Jeep
Travel home by Toyota
Travel home by Ferrari
Travel home by Tesla
Travel home by Proshe
```

What happens if there is a name of a car manufacturer like Aston Martin?

```
Travel home by Aston
Travel home by Martin
```

Again, the for command breaks the output and messes up. In order to resolve this the **field separators** were introduced.

Field Separators

A field separator can be a space, a tab, and even a new line. There is an environment variable called Internal Field Separator or IFS. This was the root cause of the previous problem. To resolve this, it is possible to define our own field separators. Let's modify the previous example by defining our own separator for the specific script.

#!/bin/bash

list="vehicles"

IFS=$'\n' #Defines our intended field separator

for vehicle in $(cat $list)

do

echo "Travel home by $vehicle"

done

```
Travel home by Aston Martin
```

It worked!

Another useful feature of the for loop is the support for wildcards. This is often used when searching for files. For instance,

for file in /home/jan/*

can be used.

While Command

While command is versatile than for and if-then-else and its somewhat of a cross between these two.

Syntax:

while test command

do

> *other commands*

done

The while loop keeps running as long as the exit code is zero. If it isn't it breaks the iterations and ends the loop.

Example:

#!/bin/bash

num1=5

while [$num1 -gt 0]

do

echo $num1

num1=$[$num1 - 1]

done

```
jan@jan-virtual-machine:~/Desktop$ ./Myscript
5
4
3
2
1
```

Until Command

This is the last of our commands. Until command can be thought of as the opposite of the *while* command.

Syntax:

until test commands

do

*   other commands*

done

Example:

```
#!/bin/bash

var1=10

until [ $var1 -eq 0 ]

do

        echo $var1

        var1=$[ $var1 - 2 ]

done
```

```
jan@jan-virtual-machine:~/Desktop$ ./Myscript
10
8
6
4
2
```

The Break and the Continue Commands

Controlling loops is an essential requirement in scripting, as well as any other programming discipline. The **break** command simply breaks a loop and exits out. This can be used with if-then-else command, while and until commands.

On the other hand, the **continue** command skips the iteration and goes to the next iteration. However, it does not break the loop entirely. We have previously used the break command and therefore, the following example is on the continue command.

```
#!/bin/bash

for i in 1 2 3 4 5 6 7 8 9

do

if [ $i -eq 5 ]

then

        echo "skipping 5th iteration..."

        continue

fi
```

echo "I is equal to $i"

done

```
jan@jan-virtual-machine:~/Desktop$ ./Myscript
"I is equal to 1"
"I is equal to 2"
"I is equal to 3"
"I is equal to 4"
"skipping 5th iteration…"
"I is equal to 6"
"I is equal to 7"
"I is equal to 8"
"I is equal to 9"
```

This concludes the lesson on structured commands and conditionals. At the end, we will look into one real-life scenario so that you can practically use what you have learned so far.

Example: Creating a Set of Users

If you have been working as an administrator, you may have already used techniques to create users using bulk updates. In such cases, we often use either text files or comma-separated files (.CSV or a spreadsheet, an Excel-like file if you are a Windows user). In this example, we will be using such a file and create multiple users. When creating users, you must access files, check whether the user exists, or not and iterate until the end of the file.

We will have the following fields in the file.

username,fn

Here, fn stands for full name.

As you already noticed, comma separated file is not align with the default field separators. In this case, we need to use our own separator.

IFS=','

In addition, we will use the read command to perform the reading from the file.

#!/bin/bash

inp="/home/jan/Desktop/users"

while IFS=',' read -r uid fn

do

echo "adding $uid"

useradd -c "$fn" -m $uid

done < $inp

```
root@jan-virtual-machine:~# /home/jan/Desktop/Myscript
adding jane
adding jake
adding smith
```

CHAPTER 9: Introduction to Functions

In this chapter you will learn

> What functions are
>
> Parameters and options
>
> getopt(s)
>
> Writing functions
>
> Handling functions (exit status, arguments, variables and arrays)
>
> GAWK basics

Before going into functions, some important topics will be discussed in this section starting with handling user input. Handling user input is essential in actual scenarios. Interactive scripts are useful when it requires to handle data and input from the user. Linux offers a few command line parameters, options as well as handling direct input (e.g., from Keyboard).

You have already come aware of how startup values are passed when executing a shell script. For instance, we executed ./Myscript with ./Myscript car value. It provided specific information for this input. This is actually an interactive script and it was able to handle user input.

Reading a supplied parameter is handled by bash. There is a special variable called **positional parameters**. These parameters handle the script name and 8 other parameters so that it can be used with custom input values. The script name is held by $0. $1 - $9 holds the rest.

Let's look at a simple mathematical equation with 2 arguments.

#!/bin/bash

*multiplication=$[$1 * $2]*

echo The multiplication of $1 and $2 is $multiplication

```
jan@jan-virtual-machine:~/Desktop$ ./Myscript 1 2
The multiplication of 1 and 2 is 2
jan@jan-virtual-machine:~/Desktop$ ./Myscript 8 9
The multiplication of 8 and 9 is 72
```

It takes $1 and $2 and perform a simple math operation.

Another example:

#!/bin/bash

var1=$USER

echo Welcome $var1

echo Wishing you a happy $1

In this example, it takes a day for $1 and present it to the user as a greeting.

```
jan@jan-virtual-machine:~/Desktop$ ./Myscript Monday
Welcome jan
Wishing you a happy Monday
```

You must enter text within double quotation marks if you wish to enter more than one word when executing scripts. Otherwise, you will run out of parameters and a messed-up output.

In the next example, we will be reading the script name and making decisions based on it. One problem exists with the $0. It may contain more than the name of the script, e.g., path. There is a command to remove the path, as well as any other values in between. The basname command comes handy in doing so.

#!/bin/bash

var1=$0

var2=$(basename $0) #Here we remove './' and other additional stuff

if [[$var2 == "Myscript"]]

then

    echo This is Jan's script $var1 #Raw name

    echo This is Jan's script without additional things in the name: $var2

    #This line returns the formatted name with basename

else

    echo This not Jan's script but $var2

fi

```
jan@jan-virtual-machine:~/Desktop$ ./Myscript
This is Jan's script ./Myscript
This is Jan's script without additional things in the name: Myscript
```

Now you know how to use script name as a variable. You can make decisions based on the script name. For instance, if a script has a name 'who' it can run the *who* command. If the name is addition, you could only execute the addition where the script can perform subtraction.

When you run the scripts with parameters, you must be sure that no inaccurate or unexpected values are passed causing crashes. Therefore, it is the best practice to test the input and pass them through if-then-else decision-making ladder. However, this is also a cumbersome task. Therefore, we could use some special parameters to assist.

Counting Parameters

There is a special variable for counting the number of parameters entered. It is

$#. This variable counts the number of parameters entered upon executing the script. Let's look at the following example.

#!/bin/bash

var1=$#

echo Number of arguments supplied $var1

```
jan@jan-virtual-machine:~/Desktop$ ./Myscript
Number of arguments supplied 0
jan@jan-virtual-machine:~/Desktop$ ./Myscript 1
Number of arguments supplied 1
jan@jan-virtual-machine:~/Desktop$ ./Myscript 1 2 3 4 5 6 7 8 9
Number of arguments supplied 9
jan@jan-virtual-machine:~/Desktop$ ./Myscript 1 2 3 4 5 6 7 8 9 10
Number of arguments supplied 10
jan@jan-virtual-machine:~/Desktop$
```

Another example: Calculating factorial if and only if the number of parameters equals to one.

#!/bin/bash

var1=$#

num=$1

if [$var1 -eq 1]

then

> *fact=1*

> *while [$num -gt 1]*

do

    *fact=$((fact * num))*

    num=$((num - 1))

    done

    echo $fact

else

    echo "Script usage: ./Myscript argument. Example: ./Myscript 5"

fi

```
jan@jan-virtual-machine:~/Desktop$ ./Myscript 5
120
jan@jan-virtual-machine:~/Desktop$ ./Myscript
Script usage: ./Myscript argument. Example: ./Myscript 5
jan@jan-virtual-machine:~/Desktop$ ./Myscript 5 4
Script usage: ./Myscript argument. Example: ./Myscript 5
```

There are two other unique variables providing a way to obtain the last parameter and script name used. These are:

- $#
- {!S#}

Let's run the following script and obtain the output.

#!/bin/bash

echo $#

echo ${!#}

```
jan@jan-virtual-machine:~/Desktop$ ./Myscript
0
./Myscript
jan@jan-virtual-machine:~/Desktop$ ./Myscript 5
1
5
jan@jan-virtual-machine:~/Desktop$ ./Myscript 5 6 7
3
7
```

To access all the parameters there are two more variables,

- $*
- $@

These two variables provide access to all the parameters in two different ways.

- $* variable provides access to all the parameters as a single line.
- $@ variables provides access to all the parameters individually.

This can be explained by using a for loop.

```
#!/bin/bash

count=1

for params in "$*"

do

        echo "Variabe \$* Parameter #$count = $params"

        count=$[ $count + 1 ]

done

echo

count=1


for params in "$@"

do

        echo "Variable \$@ Parameter #$count = $params"

        count=$[ $count + 1 ]

done
```

```
jan@jan-virtual-machine:~/Desktop$ ./Myscript
Variabe $* Parameter #1 =

jan@jan-virtual-machine:~/Desktop$ ./Myscript 56
Variabe $* Parameter #1 = 56

Variable $@ Parameter #1 = 56
jan@jan-virtual-machine:~/Desktop$ ./Myscript 56 65
Variabe $* Parameter #1 = 56 65

Variable $@ Parameter #1 = 56
Variable $@ Parameter #2 = 65
```

Shifting Things

The **shift** command is another useful command. It shifts the current positional parameters left **n** time. This n = 1 by default.

Syntax: *shift [n]*

In the next example, let's try to shift the provided values

#!/bin/bash

shift 0

echo Param 0: $0

echo Param 1: $1

echo Param 2: $2

echo Param 3: $3

echo Param 4: $4

```
jan@jan-virtual-machine:~/Desktop$ ./Myscript 1 2 3 4 5
Param 0: ./Myscript
Param 1: 1
Param 2: 2
Param 3: 3
Param 4: 4
```

Now let's start shifting them.

```
#!/bin/bash

shift 1

echo Param 0: $0

echo Param 1: $1

echo Param 2: $2

echo Param 3: $3

echo Param 4: $4
```

```
jan@jan-virtual-machine:~/Desktop$ ./Myscript 1 2 3 4 5
Param 0:  ./Myscript
Param 1:  2
Param 2:  3
Param 3:  4
Param 4:  5
```

Although the $0 has no change, the other values have been shifted. Let's use a *for* loop this time.

```
#!/bin/bash

for (( i = 0; i <= 4; i++ ));

do

        echo Shifting $i:

        echo 1: $1

        echo 2: $2

        echo 3: $3

        echo 4: $4

        shift

done
```

```
jan@jan-virtual-machine:~/Desktop$ ./Myscript 1 2 3 4 5
Shifting 0:
1:  1
2:  2
3:  3
4:  4
Shifting 1:
1:  2
2:  3
3:  4
4:  5
Shifting 2:
1:  2
2:  4
3:  5
4:
Shifting 3:
1:  4
2:  5
3:
4:
Shifting 4:
1:  5
2:
3:
4:
```

In this output, you can see how the provided values are getting shifted during the 5 iterations. If we provide 4 values, the entire values will be shifted without any number remaining.

We can use this shifting to do things like traversing folders. A practical example will be removal of files in a specific directory or directories older than 365 days.

Moving with Options

In the previous lesson we learned about passing arguments or parameters with the execution. We can also pass options. These options can be used to take decisions based on the provided options.

Let's take a look at an example.

#!/bin/bash

while [-n "$1"]

do

      case "$1" in

      -x) echo "Found a valid option -x" ;;

      -y) echo "Found a valid option -y" ;;

      -z) echo "Found a valid option -z" ;;

      *) echo "$1 is not a valid option" ;;

esac

shift

done

```
jan@jan-virtual-machine:~/Desktop$ ./Myscript
jan@jan-virtual-machine:~/Desktop$ ./Myscript -s
-s is not a valid option
jan@jan-virtual-machine:~/Desktop$ ./Myscript -x
Found a valid option -x
jan@jan-virtual-machine:~/Desktop$ ./Myscript -x -y -z -t
Found a valid option -x
Found a valid option -y
Found a valid option -z
-t is not a valid option
jan@jan-virtual-machine:~/Desktop$ ./Myscript -x -y -z -t -z
Found a valid option -x
Found a valid option -y
Found a valid option -z
-t is not a valid option
Found a valid option -z
```

If we combine the examples for finding parameters and options, we can obtain both successfully.

#!/bin/bash

while [-n "$1"]

do

> *case "$1" in*
>
> *-x) echo "Found a valid option -x" ;;*
>
> *-y) echo "Found a valid option -y" ;;*
>
> *-z) echo "Found a valid option -z" ;;*
>
> **) echo "$1 is not a valid option" ;;*
>
> *esac*
>
> *shift*

count=1

for params in "$@"

do

    echo "Variabe \\$@ Parameter #$count = $params"

    count=$[$count + 1]

done

echo

done

Using getopt and getopts Commands

These two commands are used to parse or break the options provided through the command line.

Syntax of getopt: *getopts optstring name [argument]…*

There are few things to note before we get into the actual use of getopt.

-    optstring: Defines valid option letters used in the CLI.
-    This also defines which of these letters require a parameter value.
-    Either '+' or '-' must be used when providing options. As soon as we provide the number of options or an option with no + or − then the command ends processing the list.

To use this, we have to follow some rules. When you supply a list of options, you must use colons to notify an option has one or more parameters.

Let's take a look at an example. Here, we define the input pattern as

getopt ab:c:d

This means we are going to provide an option -a (or +a), then an option -b with a parameter (i.e. -b param1), then -c (e.g., -c param2 param3) and -d.

```
jan@jan-virtual-machine:~/Desktop$ getopt ab:c:d -ab param1 -c param2 param3 -d
 -a -b param1 -c param2 -d -- param3
```

As you see at the end of -d it stops processing the options.

You must have seen the param1 and param2 are experiencing an issue. When the parameters have spaces between it, there is a problem. However, if we ignore it for now, we can do some more experiments.

```
jan@jan-virtual-machine:~/Desktop$ getopt ab:c:d -ab param1 -c param2 -d
 -a -b param1 -c param2 -d --
jan@jan-virtual-machine:~/Desktop$ getopt ab:c:d -ab param1 -c param2 param3
 -a -b param1 -c param2 -- param3
jan@jan-virtual-machine:~/Desktop$ getopt ab:c:d -ab param1 c param2
 -a -b param1 -- c param2
jan@jan-virtual-machine:~/Desktop$ getopt ab:c:d -ab param1 -c param2 -d -e
getopt: invalid option -- 'e'
 -a -b param1 -c param2 -d --
```

Also, note that -ab is treated as -a -b (is fine in this example). The first example is the normal operation. In the second, we do not provide a -d and it terminates the line at param3. In the second, it is terminated at param1 as c has lost its '-'. Finally, we provide an additional option and it was rejected successfully.

There are some options with getopt itself.

```
Options:
 -a, --alternative           allow long options starting with single -
 -l, --longoptions <longopts>  the long options to be recognized
 -n, --name <progname>       the name under which errors are reported
 -o, --options <optstring>   the short options to be recognized
 -q, --quiet                 disable error reporting by getopt(3)
 -Q, --quiet-output          no normal output
 -s, --shell <shell>         set quoting conventions to those of <shell>
 -T, --test                  test for getopt(1) version
 -u, --unquoted              do not quote the output

 -h, --help                  display this help
 -V, --version               display version
```

Example: Parsing Options with getopt

Source: https://gist.github.com/cosimo/3760587

(with extra clarify and output)

#!/bin/bash

ARGS=`getopt -o vhns: --long verbose,dry-run,help,stack-size: -n 'parse-options' -- "$@"`

#Parse parameters and store normalized strings in $ARGS. We are using getopt options -o, --long, and -n for error reporting

if [$? != 0] ; then echo "Failed parsing options." >&2 ; exit 1 ; fi

```
#If the command has not exited with 0 = error


echo "$ARGS"

#Echoes the provided options and parameter if any

eval set -- "$ARGS"

#Set parameters to pre-processed string $ARGS

VERBOSE=false

HELP=false

DRY_RUN=false

STACK_SIZE=0


while true; do
        case "$1" in
                -v | --verbose ) VERBOSE=true; shift ;;
                -h | --help )    HELP=true; shift ;;
                -n | --dry-run ) DRY_RUN=true; shift ;;
                -s | --stack-size ) STACK_SIZE="$2"; shift; shift ;;
                -- ) shift; break ;;
                * ) break ;;
        esac
done


echo VERBOSE=$VERBOSE

echo HELP=$HELP

echo DRY_RUN=$DRY_RUN
```

echo STACK_SIZE=$STACK_SIZE

```
jan@jan-virtual-machine:~/Desktop$ ./Myscript -v
 -v --
VERBOSE=true
HELP=false
DRY_RUN=false
STACK_SIZE=0
jan@jan-virtual-machine:~/Desktop$ ./Myscript -vhns
parse-options: option requires an argument -- 's'
Failed parsing options.
jan@jan-virtual-machine:~/Desktop$ ./Myscript -vhns 5
 -v -h -n -s '5' --
VERBOSE=true
HELP=true
DRY_RUN=true
STACK_SIZE=5
jan@jan-virtual-machine:~/Desktop$ ./Myscript -vhns 5 6
 -v -h -n -s '5' -- '6'
VERBOSE=true
HELP=true
DRY_RUN=true
STACK_SIZE=5
jan@jan-virtual-machine:~/Desktop$ ./Myscript -vsd -5
parse-options: invalid option -- '5'
Failed parsing options.
jan@jan-virtual-machine:~/Desktop$ ./Myscript -vsd
 -v -s 'd' --
VERBOSE=true
HELP=false
DRY_RUN=false
STACK_SIZE=d
jan@jan-virtual-machine:~/Desktop$ ./Myscript -vh -s 5
 -v -h -s '5' --
VERBOSE=true
HELP=true
DRY_RUN=false
STACK_SIZE=5
```

The outputs of this screenshot are as follows.

1. Normal operation example.
2. Failed as the value is missing for stack size.
3. With full options and parameter value provided.
4. Extra parameter value rejected.
5. Passed d as the size (it should check for numbers) and a '-5' that is invalid.
6. Another normal operation with 3 options and a parameter value.

As you understand, there are several issues with *getopt*. The most prevailing is the multiple parameter values and its inability to detect two or more as a single set when separated with a spacebar. Even if we use "" getopt simply does not detect a difference.

getopts to the Rescue

There are two important implicit variables (environment variables) of getopts. Those are,

- $OPTIND.
- $OPTARG.

$OPTIND (OPTion INDex) is the argument pointer to the flags (e.g., -a). The $OPTARG (OPTional ARGuments) is the optional arguments attached to a flag (e.g., -a test).

There are few other rules.

- If a letter is followed by a ';' it takes the option as having a parameter value.
- If the command starts with ':'
- If options provided without '-' or '+' will stop the processing.
- When the while command is used with this, it does not need brackets.

Example: In this example, we will use *getopts* to obtain the checksum of a file from an algorithm selection.

```
jan@jan-virtual-machine:~/Desktop$ ./Myscript -m ./Myscript
MD5 Selected
------------------------------
41513791e410a59a8923383b50101c11  -
------------------------------
jan@jan-virtual-machine:~/Desktop$ md5sum ./Myscript
41513791e410a59a8923383b50101c11  ./Myscript
jan@jan-virtual-machine:~/Desktop$ sha1sum ./Myscript
9a17381222988798c74f3b85c67ba8f45495e9bc  ./Myscript
jan@jan-virtual-machine:~/Desktop$ ./Myscript -s ./Myscript
SHA1 Selected
------------------------------
9a17381222988798c74f3b85c67ba8f45495e9bc  -
------------------------------
jan@jan-virtual-machine:~/Desktop$ ./Myscript -h
Usage= Myscript options [-m filename] [-s filename] -h for help. Example: ./Mysc
ript -m File1.txt
```

This is the output compared with running the commands individually.

#!/bin/bash

USAGE="Usage= `basename $0` options [-m filename] [-s filename] -h for help. Example: ./Myscript -m File1.txt"

FILENAME_M="   #This argument is provided with -m

FILENAME_S="   #This argument is provided with -s

SEL="   #Records the selection from m, s or h

```
while getopts "m:s:h" opt; do          #After m or s there must be a following value
        case "$opt" in
                m) FILENAME_M="$OPTARG"          #Assigns the optional value
                echo "MD5 Selected"
                SEL=$opt                          #SEL=m
                ;;
                s) FILENAME_S="$OPTARG"  #Assigns the optional value
                echo "SHA1 Selected"
                SEL=$opt                          #SEL=s
                ;;
                h) echo $USAGE && exit 0;;
        esac
done
shift $(( OPTIND - 1 ))
if [[ $SEL == m ]] && [[ $FILENAME_M == '' ]]; then              #If no filename
                                                                 #provided.
        echo "YOU MUST PROVIDE A FILE NAME!X $USAGE" >&2
        exit 1
elif [[ $SEL == m ]] && [[ $FILENAME_M != '' ]]; then    #If m with filename
        echo ----------------------------
        md5sum < $FILENAME_M
        echo ----------------------------
elif [[ $SEL == s ]] && [[ $FILENAME_S == '' ]]; then            #If s without a
                                                                 #filename
        echo "YOU MUST PROVIDE A FILE NAME!Y $USAGE" >&2
        exit 1
```

```
elif [[ $SEL == s ]] && [[ $FILENAME_S != '' ]]; then          #If s with filename

        echo ----------------------------

        sha1sum < $FILENAME_S

        echo ----------------------------
else

        echo "Unable to proceed: $USAGE"

fi
```

Reading User Input

The most important interactive feature of a script or any program is taking the user input and process it to create an effective and accurate output. To read user input in the Linux world we use the **read** command. This command offers a set of comprehensive options and can be used for advanced operations.

Syntax: *read [-ers] [-a array] [-d delim] [-i text] [-n nchars] [-N nchars]*

*   *[-p prompt] [-t timeout] [-u fd] [name ...] [name2 ...]*

Table 9.1: read command options

-a array	Assign the words read to sequential indices of the array variable ARRAY, starting at zero
-d delim	Continue until the first character of DELIM is read, rather than newline
-e	use Readline to obtain the line in an interactive shell
-i text	Use TEXT as the initial text for Readline
-n nchars	Return after reading NCHARS characters rather than waiting for a newline, but honor a delimiter if fewer than NCHARS characters are read before the delimiter
-N nchars	Return only after reading exactly NCHARS characters, unless EOF is encountered or read times out, ignoring any delimiter

-p prompt	Output the string PROMPT without a trailing newline before attempting to read
-r	Do not allow backslashes to escape any characters
-s	Do not echo input coming from a terminal
-t timeout	Time out and return failure if a complete line of input is not read within t TIMEOUT seconds. The value of the TMOUT variable is the default timeout. TIMEOUT may be a fractional number. If TIMEOUT is 0, read returns success only if input is available on the specified file descriptor. The exit status is greater than 128 if the timeout is exceeded
-u fd	Read from file descriptor FD instead of the standard input

Now, let's try some examples and learn how to use the command.

#!/bin/bash

echo -n "Enter your name: "

read name

echo "Hi $name, welcome to Ubuntu GNOME desktop. "

```
jan@jan-virtual-machine:~/Desktop$ ./Myscript
Enter your name: Jan
Hi Jan, welcome to Ubuntu GNOME desktop.
```

Pretty cool! Isn't it? The next example uses the *-p* option.

#!/bin/bash

read -p "Enter your name: " name

echo "Hi $name, welcome to Ubuntu GNOME desktop. "

```
jan@jan-virtual-machine:~/Desktop$ ./Myscript
Enter your name: Jake
Hi Jake, welcome to Ubuntu GNOME desktop.
```

In this example, we were using a variable. However, even if you do not specify one, the read command has its own environment variable *REPLY* to hold such data.

Example:

#!/bin/bash

read -p "Enter your name: "

echo "Hi $REPLY, welcome to Ubuntu GNOME desktop. "

```
jan@jan-virtual-machine:~/Desktop$ ./Myscript
Enter your name: John
Hi John, welcome to Ubuntu GNOME desktop.
```

Another useful option is the **-t** option. We can use this to expire the user input prompt.

#!/bin/bash

if read -t 30 -p "Enter your name: "

then

       echo "Hi $REPLY, welcome to Ubuntu GNOME desktop. "

else

       echo "Your session timed out! :("

fi

```
jan@jan-virtual-machine:~/Desktop$ ./Myscript
Enter your name: Jan
Hi Jan, welcome to Ubuntu GNOME desktop.
jan@jan-virtual-machine:~/Desktop$ ./Myscript
Enter your name: Your session timed out! :(
```

If you were unable to respond within 30 seconds, the read will automatically terminate. It is like a session timeout isn't it?

Reading passwords is also possible with read, and the cool thing is, it can stop displaying the characters we type.

```
#!/bin/bash
read -p "Enter your name: "
echo "Hi $REPLY, welcome to Ubuntu GNOME desktop. "
read -s -p "Enter your password: " pass
echo "Your password is $pass"
```

```
jan@jan-virtual-machine:~/Desktop$ ./Myscript
Enter your name: Jan
Hi Jan, welcome to Ubuntu GNOME desktop.
Enter your password: "Your password is J@n2019"
```

It is also possible to read single characters (i.e., Y/N) and it can be useful when requesting a confirmation from the user. For this case, you can integrate it with the case command.

Finally, we will read from a file and add some line numbers to make read convenient.

```
#!/bin/bash
fName="          #To store the filename the user inputs
count=1          #Otherwise, the count starts from 0
read -p "File name: "
fName=$REPLY
echo $fName
cat $fName | while read line
        do
                echo "$count: $line"
                count=$[ $count + 1]
        done
echo "EOF"
```

```
jan@jan-virtual-machine:~/Desktop$ ./Myscript
File name: File3.txt
File3.txt
1: MAR
2: NOV
3: DEC
4: APR
5: FEB
6: APR
EOF
```

Writing Functions

When you are handling tasks using small to large scripts, it is a tedious task to continuously rewrite the code when parts of the code can be reused in the same script or somewhere else. Instead, it is great if such parts can be reused or recalled with necessary values. This is common in general programing platforms. Well, bash is not a loser here! It offers the same and is called a **function.**

Functions are code blocks that can be reused in a script. In this section you will learn how to use functions in your code.

Basic Components

A function can be defined in the following way. It is not complicated.

function function_name {

commands

}

Let's test the function of a function in an example.

#!/bin/bash

function love {

echo "Do you love Linux?"

}

for((x=1; x<=5; x++))

do

love

done

```
jan@jan-virtual-machine:~/Desktop$ ./Myscript
Do you love Linux?
Do you love Linux?
Do you love Linux?
Do you love Linux?
Do you love Linux?
```

The function is called within the loop and it works!

What would happen if we create a function and change the definition of the same function (both functions will have the same name) elsewhere below the code from the first function?

Then the names will be the same, yet **it will use the 2ⁿᵈ definition**!

Exit Status and Return Value

A function should have an exist status. However, since it can have many commands and success/failures, it will return the last successful or unsuccessful status. This may become troublesome although we can query is by '$?'.

This is where the return value of a function becomes useful. Let's look at an example.

#!/bin/bash

function calculate   *{*

        num1=0

        num2=0

        cal=0

        read -p "Input your first value: " num1

        read -p "Input your second value: " num2

        cal=$[$num1 + $num2]

        echo $cal

        return 0

        }

calculate

echo "$?"

echo "The end!"

```
jan@jan-virtual-machine:~/Desktop$ ./Myscript
Input your first value: 6
Input your second value: 9
15
0
The end!
```

There are 2 limitations to this technique, however. Those are:

- You must not execute any command before capturing the exit status.
- You must use a return value below 256 that is a limitation of the return value.

To resolve this problem, we can directly obtain the return value by following this procedure.

#!/bin/bash

var1=100

var2=200

var3=0

var_F=0

function math {

        var3=$[$var1 + $var2]

        echo $var3

}

echo "The return value is being calculated..."

var_F=$(math)

echo "The result is $var_F"

```
jan@jan-virtual-machine:~/Desktop$ ./Myscript
The return value is being calculated...
"The result is 300"
```

Passing Arguments

Just like we did with scripts, we can pass variables to functions. The function can use $1 to $9 variables to capture the values. The function can retrieve these values and execute the commands.

#!/bin/bash

function calculate

{

    if [$# -eq 0] || [$# -gt 2]

    then

        echo "Need two values!"

    elif [$# -eq 1]

    then

        echo "Need one more value"

    else

        echo $[$1 + $2]

    fi

}

val=$(calculate 250 500)

echo $val

echo "The end!"

```
jan@jan-virtual-machine:~/Desktop$ ./Myscript
750
The end!
```

In this example, we have passed 2 simple arguments. Then we took each argument and performed a calculation. If you still remember how to use $1- $9 this is a simple task.

Handling Variables

In the next section, we will look at how environment variables can be integrated with functions.

Using variables in a function is essential. However, when you use functions you must be careful of one thing. Do not use the same name for variables inside the function, as well as outside, because one can corrupt the data of the other. To avoid such issues, you could use **local** and **global** variables.

Let's look at this example.

```
#!/bin/bash

function compare

{

        temp=10

        result=$[ $temp+1 ]

}

temp=5

compare

echo "Final result =" $result

if [ $temp -eq 10 ]; then

        echo "Compromised!"

else

        echo "Not compromised!"

fi
```

```
jan@jan-virtual-machine:~/Desktop$ ./Myscript
Final result = 11
Compromised!
```

Now you see the problem here. The temp variable is assigned a value 5. Yet after the execution of the function it is 10. Let's try with a local variable this time.

```
#!/bin/bash

function compare
```

```
{

        local temp=10

        result=$[ $temp+1 ]

}

temp=5

compare

echo "Final result =" $result

if [ $temp -eq 10 ]; then

        echo "Compromised!"

elif [ $temp -eq 5 ]; then

        echo "Not compromised!"

else

        echo -1

fi
```

```
jan@jan-virtual-machine:~/Desktop$ ./Myscript
Final result = 11
Not compromised!
```

Now, temp is 5 and there is no conflict.

Using Arrays and Passing Arrays

If you are familiar with arrays, you may know what it is. However, for a reader who isn't familiar with arrays, this section includes an introduction.

An array is a memory location that we construct to hold more than one parameter. We can create arrays in two ways.

- By declaring an array.
- By creating an array.

Declaring an Array

To declare an array, we can simply use the following syntax.

declare -a my_array

Create an Array on the Fly

The following syntax can be used to create an array on the fly.

my_array=(foo baz)

Handling Arrays

To insert or modify a value, we could,

my_array[0]=foo

We have inserted foo as the first element of this array.

To retrieve data, we could use the following methods.

- echo ${my_array[@]} : Using the @ symbol
- echo ${my_array[*]} : Using the * symbol.

```
jan@jan-virtual-machine:~/Desktop$ my_array=(foo baz)
jan@jan-virtual-machine:~/Desktop$ echo ${my_array[*]}
foo baz
jan@jan-virtual-machine:~/Desktop$ echo ${my_array[@]}
foo baz
```

I hope you remember the difference between the @ and *. Let's look at this using a for loop.

#!/bin/bash

my_array=(foo baz)

for x in "${my_array[@]}"

do

        echo "$x";

done

for y in "${my_array[*]}"

do

        echo "$y";

done

```
jan@jan-virtual-machine:~/Desktop$ ./Myscript
foo
baz
foo baz
```

As you see, the @ returns each element and the other returns all items, but in a single string.

Using Arrays in Functions

Using arrays in functions can be very useful as the code can be reused due to the complexity arrays introduce. Let's learn from an example.

```
#!/bin/bash

function arr_test

{
        local temp_arr

        temp_arr=("$@")                #Assigns values to the array from the outside.

        echo "Value of the array in the function is: ${temp_arr[*]}"

}


my_array=(a b c d e)

echo "Array values in the original array is: ${my_array[*]}"

arr_test ${my_array[*]}
```

> **Note**: You could either use '@' or '*'.

```
jan@jan-virtual-machine:~/Desktop$ ./Myscript
Array values in the original array is: a b c d e
Value of the array in the function is: a b c d e
```

As you see, the two arrays have identical values.

Recursive Functions

What is a recursion? A function may call itself for certain purposes. The best example is calculating factorial. When calculating, the function recursively call itself to run the calculations. Let's look at this example.

```
#!/bin/bash

function factorial {

if [ $1 -eq 1 ]            #If the input is 1, then the result is one

then

        echo 1

else                       #If the input is not 1 then

        local tmp=$[ $1 - 1 ]

        local result=$(factorial $tmp) #The function calls itself again

        echo $[ $result * $1 ]

fi

}

read -p "Enter value: "

result=$(factorial $REPLY)

echo "The factorial of $value is: $result"
```

```
jan@jan-virtual-machine:~/Desktop$ ./Myscript
Enter value: 1
The factorial of  is: 1
jan@jan-virtual-machine:~/Desktop$ ./Myscript
Enter value: 2
The factorial of  is: 2
jan@jan-virtual-machine:~/Desktop$ ./Myscript
Enter value: 3
The factorial of  is: 6
jan@jan-virtual-machine:~/Desktop$ ./Myscript
Enter value: 4
The factorial of  is: 24
jan@jan-virtual-machine:~/Desktop$ ./Myscript
Enter value: 5
The factorial of  is: 120
```

Using Function as a Library

We have already learned about how functions can be used efficiently. However, you cannot still use a function outside the original script because it is limited to the current session. Is it the truth? No! You can use functions in a script for a purpose of another. Here is how.

You simply have to save the script in the same location as the script trying to use it. Or else, you need to provide the full (absolute) path. There is also a proper way to call an external script. Let's learn it in the following code.

#!/bin/bash

function add {

> *echo $[$1 + $2]*

}

This is our script and let's save it as *custom_func*

Now, let's invoke in it another script saved in the same location.

#!/bin/bash

. ./custom_func

num1=10

num2=20

result=$(add $num1 $num2)

echo $result

```
jan@jan-virtual-machine:~/Desktop$ ./Myscript
30
```

Finally, we are successfully able to store out library and reuse it as we have always wanted!

This chapter has covered fundamentals and advanced uses of functions and how a function can be used in different perspectives. This section will not cover graphics interfaces as it would be too advanced for a starter.

Introduction to GAWK

In order to do data and file manipulation you could use bash shell and SED to perform certain advanced functions. However, to manipulate data, especially complex data, you often need an environment similar to a programing environment. This is where you would go for AWK.

The name "AWK" had derived from the 3 authors who wrote this program, **Alfred Aho, Peter Weinberger, and Brian Kernighan**.

GWAK is AWK's GNU version. It addresses certain limitations in editors like SED. It isn't just a command editor. It has its own programming language and can do much more including the following.

- Define variables and store data using the variables.
- Arithmetic and string operations.
- Structured programing capabilities.
- Data formatting and reorganizing for reporting purposes.

The last feature is highly important when there is a large set of data files, such as logs and when reports have to be generated from these data with various views. GAWK is able to format the data into more readable and understanding information that makes sense. The entire GAWK manual is available at https://www.gnu.org/software/gawk/manual/gawk.html

GAWK Options
Syntax:

gawk [POSIX or GNU style options] -f program-file [--] file ...

gawk [POSIX or GNU style options] [--] program-text file ...

pgawk [POSIX or GNU style options] -f program-file [--] file ...

pgawk [POSIX or GNU style options] [--] program-text file ...

dgawk [POSIX or GNU style options] -f program-file [--] file ...

A gawk program looks like the following.

> pattern { action }

> pattern { action }

Let's try our first gawk lesson with the **print** command.

Example: *gawk '{print "Hello World!"}'*

Or else, you could also use **mawk** in Ubuntu.

Example: *mawk '{print "Hello World!"}'*

Terminating GAWK
Once you run the gawk program you need know how to end it. It accepts **Ctrl+D** as the terminate signal. By pressing it will stop the gawk.

Another example:

awk '{ print "Don\47t Panic!" }'

```
jan@jan-virtual-machine:~/Desktop$ awk '{print "Hello World!"}'
Hello World!
```

Note the escape characters. You cannot use the symbol ' here.

Another instance is when you wish to print first word of each line of a log file. Remember, do not use ' symbol as you normally would with other programming languages.

awk '{print $1}' log.   #The log. is the file name

```
jan@jan-virtual-machine:~/Desktop$ cat log.
jan         :0              2019-09-24 03:42 (:0)
jan@jan-virtual-machine:~/Desktop$ awk '{print $1}' log.
jan
```

In order to change the field separator, use the **-F** option.

```
jan@jan-virtual-machine:~/Desktop$ cat log.
jan      :0           2019-09-24 03:42 (:0)
jan@jan-virtual-machine:~/Desktop$ awk -F '{print $1}' log.
awk: 1: unexpected character '.'
jan@jan-virtual-machine:~/Desktop$ awk -F: '{print $1}' log.
jan
jan@jan-virtual-machine:~/Desktop$ awk -F- '{print $1}' log.
jan      :0           2019
```

We are using no separators at first and then ':' and '-' as separators in next steps.

When you use *awk* in the command-line, you could start with *awk* '{ and press enter. Then it will start accepting your commands until you enter the single quotation symbol '.

Another advanced feature of gawk is the ability to store a program in a file and refer in the CLI.

- Let's create a new awk files in the desktop and name it *script.awk*.
- Let's have it read the $1 and $6 of a file and echo the content.
- *{print "The user "$1"'s home directory is:" $6}*
- Save the file.
- Now, run the following command
- *awk -F: -f ./script.awk /etc/passwd*

```
jan@jan-virtual-machine:~/Desktop$ cat script.awk
{print "The user "$1"'s home directory is:" $6}
jan@jan-virtual-machine:~/Desktop$ awk -F: -f ./script.awk /etc/passwd
The user root's home directory is:/root
The user daemon's home directory is:/usr/sbin
The user bin's home directory is:/bin
The user sys's home directory is:/dev
The user sync's home directory is:/bin
The user games's home directory is:/usr/games
The user man's home directory is:/var/cache/man
The user lp's home directory is:/var/spool/lpd
```

In this example, we call the script and pass the file /etc/passwd. The other script takes it, uses the delimiter ':' and breaks the 1st and 6th fields.

jan:x:1000:1000:Jan,,,:/home/jan:/bin/bash

   (1)   (6)

   (2)

Understanding Data Fields

Now you have a basic understanding of how gawk or awk works. In order to utilize the data fields properly, you need to know how the field variables work.

- $0 represents the entire line.
- $1 represents the first data field.
- $n represents the last data field.

This is how you should access data by using these variables.

Processing GAWK Before Processing Data

In any software program, you find welcoming and instructional lines before the start. It is difficult in GAWK without a special variable BEGIN. In the following example, it is demonstrated.

Example: *awk 'BEGIN {print "Hello World!"}'*

```
jan@jan-virtual-machine:~/Desktop$ awk 'BEGIN {print "Hello World!"}'
Hello World!
```

Processing the End of File

As BEGIN starts the process before processing data, END keyword allows you to specify a script once the reading of data ends.

awk 'BEGIN {print "File Contents:"}

{print $0}

END {print "End of File"}' File3.txt

```
jan@jan-virtual-machine:~/Desktop$ ./script.awk
File Contents:
MAR
NOV
DEC
APR
FEB
APR
End of File
```

GAWK Variables

Just like we used variables, GAWK also facilitate the use of variables. There are 2 types of variables.

- User-defined Variables.

- Built-in Variables.

Let's first look at the Built-in variables.

GAWK provides a small set of data fields and records variables. These can be utilized with both input and output data to control data and record handling. The following table includes the set.

Table 9.2: GAWK field and record variables

Variable	Usage
FIELDWIDTH	This defines the width of each data field. It is separated by spaces.
FS	Input Field Separator character
OFS	Output Field Separator character
ORS	Output Record Separator character
RS	Input Record Separator character

Let's look at the following examples using these variables.

- awk 'BEGIN{FS=":"} {print $1 "\t" $5}' /etc/passwd

```
jan       Jan,,,
test2     Testing Manager,,123-123-1234,,Technical Support Manager
q
jane      Jane Russle
jake      Jake Goldberg
smith     Smith Andarson
```

- awk 'BEGIN{FIELDWIDTHS="1 2 3 1"}{print $1,$2,$3,$4}' myfie
  This sets the field widths to 1 2 3 1
- awk 'BEGIN{FS="\n"; RS=""} {print $1,$4}' myfile
  This has the field separator 'newline' character. It prints the 1st and 4th lines of a data block such as a person's address block.

User-defined Variables

We can use our own variables when scripting with gawk. The following is a simple example of how easy it is used.

awk '

BEGIN{

    show="This is a test"

    print show

}'

```
jan@jan-virtual-machine:~/Desktop$ ./script.awk
This is a test
```

Working with Array

GAWK also allows you to work with arrays by simple means.

Syntax: *var[index] = element*

Example:

awk 'BEGIN{

    var[1] = 10

    var[2] = 50

    sum = var[1] + var[2]

    print sum

> }'

This can also be used with any string value.

```
jan@jan-virtual-machine:~/Desktop$ ./script.awk
60
```

If is also possible to iterate with arrays using the for function in an even simpler form.

Syntax:

for (var in array)

{

statements

}

Example:

awk 'BEGIN{

       test["a"] = 1

       test["b"] = 2

       test["c"] = 3

for (var in test)

{

       print var," : Value:",test[var]

}

}'

```
jan@jan-virtual-machine:~/Desktop$ ./script.awk
a   : Value: 1
b   : Value: 2
c   : Value: 3
```

To delete an array variable, there is the delete command.

Syntax: *delete array[index]*

GAWK Structured Commands

Similar to the bash scripts, gawk provides similar support for structured commands, such as if, while, do-while, and for commands. The following is the syntax and example for each command.

IF Statement

Syntax:

if {

       (condition)

}

statement1

Example:

awk '{

if ($1 > 50)

{

>   *print $1*

}

}' File3.txt

```
jan@jan-virtual-machine:~/Desktop$ ./script.awk
60
70
80
90
```

In this example, the program outputs the numbers greater than 50 from File3.txt.

While Loop

This statement has the following syntax.

while (condition)

{

statements

}

While the condition is true, it will evaluate the loop and do the required tasks.

Example:

awk '{

sum = 0

i = 1

while (i < 10)

{

    sum += $i

    i++

}

print sum

}' File3.txt

```
jan@jan-virtual-machine:~/Desktop$ ./script.awk
450
```

Do While Loop

This is similar to the while statement. However, the statement is evaluated before the while condition is met.

Syntax:

do

{

    statements

} while (condition)

For Loop

For statement in gawk is similar to the C style for loop.

Syntax: *for(variable; condition; iteration)*

Example:

awk '{

sum = 0

for (i=0; i < 10; i++)

{

    sum += $i

}

print sum

}' File3.txt

```
jan@jan-virtual-machine:~/Desktop$ ./script.awk
460
```

GAWK Functions

The most important feature of the gawk is its support for functions. There are built-in functions, as well as user-defined functions.

Built-in Functions

Gawk provides a rich set of built-in functions including the followings.

- Mathematical Functions.
- String Functions.

If you love mathematics, gawk is able to entertain you with its rich set of mathematical functions.

Mathematical Functions

The following table includes the built-in mathematical functions. Using these functions are quite simple.

Table: GAWK mathematical functions

Source: https://www.gnu.org/software/gawk/manual/html_node/Numeric-Functions.html

Function	Description
atan2(y, x)	Return the arctangent of y / x in radians. You can use 'pi = atan2(0, -1)' to retrieve the value of pi.
cos(x)	Return the cosine of x, with x in radians.
exp(x)	Return the exponential of x (e ^ x) or report an error if x is out of range. The range of values x can have depends on your machine's floating-point representation.
int(x)	Return the nearest integer to x, located between x and zero and truncated toward zero. For example, int(3) is 3, int(3.9) is 3, int(-3.9) is -3, and int(-3) is -3 as well.

log(x)	Return the natural logarithm of x, if x is positive; otherwise, return NaN ("not a number") on IEEE 754 systems. Additionally, gawk prints a warning message when x is negative.
rand()	Return a random number. The values of rand() are uniformly distributed between zero and one. The value could be zero but is never one
sin(x)	Return the sine of x, with x in radians.
sqrt(x)	Return the positive square root of x. gawk prints a warning message if x is negative. Thus, sqrt(4) is 2.
srand([x])	Set the starting point, or seed, for generating random numbers to the value x.

Example: *awk 'BEGIN{x=sqrt(16); print x}'*

```
jan@jan-virtual-machine:~/Desktop$ awk 'BEGIN{x=sqrt(16); print x}'
4
```

String Functions

There are several useful string functions and the following table includes these functions with a description.

Table: GAWK string functions

String Function
index(big, little)
length or length()
length(string)
match(string, regex)
split(string, array, separator)
split(string, array)
sprintf(format, ...)
sub(regex, subst, string)
sub(regex, subst)

gsub(regex, subst)
gsub(regex, subst, string)
substr(string, start, end)
substr(string, start)
tolower(string)
toupper(string)

Table: GAWK string parameters

Parameters	Description
big	The string that is scanned for "little"
end	Index to end the substring
format	printf format string
little	The string that is scanned for "big"
regex	Regex stands for extended regular expression
start	Where the substring started in the index
string	A string parameter.

subset

An example: *awk 'BEGIN{x = "Linux Lovers"; print toupper(x)}'*

```
jan@jan-virtual-machine:~/Desktop$ ./script.awk
LINUX LOVERS
```

User-defined Functions

As with bash scripting, gawk provides support for user-defined functions and that is not all! It supports function libraries. The following is the syntax for a function that you can define in your code.

Syntax:

function name([variables])

{

statements

}

Example:

awk '

function printing()

{

      printf "%s has the home path at %s\n", $1,$6

}

BEGIN{FS=":"}

{

      printing()

}' /etc/passwd

```
jan has the home path at /home/jan
test2 has the home path at /home/test2
q has the home path at /home/q
jane has the home path at /home/jane
jake has the home path at /home/jake
smith has the home path at /home/smith
```

This is a similar example we executed before. This uses /etc/passwd file and format it so that it will display the user's name and home directory.

Creating a Library

This is the final section of the gawk, as well as the book. In this section, you will learn how to create a functions library and use it with a different script. As you learned before, let's learn this practically. Let's revisit the /etc/passwd example.

1. Creating the library file: Create and save this file as *awkflib* on your desktop.

function myprint()

{

printf "%s has the home path at %s\n", $1,$6

}

2. Create the new script: Now, create the actual file to use this as a library and save this as script.awk

BEGIN{FS=":"}

{

   myprint()

}

3. Run the scripts.

Command: *awk -f awkflib -f script.awk /etc/passwd*

```
jan@jan-virtual-machine:~/Desktop$ awk -f awkflib -f script.awk /etc/passwd
root has the home path at /root
```

```
jan has the home path at /home/jan
test2 has the home path at /home/test2
q has the home path at /home/q
jane has the home path at /home/jane
jake has the home path at /home/jake
smith has the home path at /home/smith
```

The command was quite a success and our library file work as expected.

With this lesson you have successfully completed all the chapters and lessons in this book

Conclusion

Linux is gaining a rapid popularity among the enterprise users, as well as in schools, at home, and is used almost everywhere including servers, computers, mobile devices, IoT and countless other occasions. The content of this book will be a great source for Linux newbies and enthusiasts.

You may have not familiar with Linux yet but I invite you to try as many practice examples as possible in a Linux box. It is not difficult to find a low-cost computer to install Linux as it is not resource-hungry. Getting your hands dirty is essential.

You may have a Windows background and may find it difficult at some stages. There are many ways to change the Linux box to a Windows-like environment and the all the required information is included in this book. There are some debate about which operating system is the best. I suggest you not to go toward any judgement and learn what you have to so that you can master Linux as much as possible.

If you are willing to take professional certifications there are many paths. Learning Linux for carrier advancement is a good decision as there are many opportunities in all over the world. Red Hat offers a great set of certifications on their enterprise platform. More information on Red Hat certification can be found here: https://www.redhat.com/en/services/training-and-certification.

I have added multiple references in the book to help you get more information. Linux man pages and --help command are excellent sources as well.

The next two books will provide even more knowledge in Linux and are intended to cover all the aspects providing you with a high-level technical knowledge of Linux.

Until then, I wish all the readers good luck and happy coding!